Corporate Strategy (Remastered) I

Since 2000, more than half of the Fortune 500 companies have either gone bankrupt, been acquired, or are experiencing stagnation or decline as a result of extreme digital and social disruption. In recognition of this dilemma, *Corporate Strategy (Remastered)* was developed and designed to assist even the most experienced strategy practitioner tackle disruption and all aspects of change head on. This is the first book in the series; it provides a prescriptive solution to the way all approaches to strategy should be practiced. It embodies a context we refer to as Third Wave Strategy and its construct, a fully integrated Strategic Management Framework. The second volume is a fieldbook; it describes the methods and means to ensure successful implementation.

An illustration of Third Wave Strategy in practice is reflected in a description of strategy deployed by the highly successful Amazon corporation. Many of the components of strategy that are included in the framework will already be familiar to the reader, while others are very new. Each of the individual components discussed are supported by examples drawn from real-life case studies. The overall value of the book is its representation of a fresh, holistic, dynamic and systemic approach to strategy in a format that, frankly, hasn't existed before.

In this book, readers are also introduced to many of the soft/human elements of strategy – the primary components that make it work. Examples of topics addressed include open strategy; communities of strategy practice; reframing; sponsive strategic thinking; systemic, cognitive strategy practice; organisational learning; and strategic business intelligence.

Paul Hunter (DBA) is Founder and CEO of the Strategic Management Institute (www.smiknowledge.com) and past partner at PwC. He works on a global stage consulting and teaching. He is also the author of *The Seven Inconvenient Truths of Business Strategy* (2014) and a chapter contributor in *Corporate Universities: Drivers of the Learning Organization* (Rademakers, 2014).

Corporate Strategy (Remastered) I

High Performance Strategy and Leadership in a Volatile, Disrupted World

Paul Hunter

Routledge
Taylor & Francis Group

LONDON AND NEW YORK

First published 2021
by Routledge
2 Park Square, Milton Park, Abingdon, Oxon OX14 4RN

and by Routledge
52 Vanderbilt Avenue, New York, NY 10017

Routledge is an imprint of the Taylor & Francis Group, an informa business

© 2021 Paul Hunter

British Library Cataloguing-in-Publication Data
A catalogue record for this book is available from the British Library

Library of Congress Cataloging-in-Publication Data
Names: Hunter, Paul Wilson, 1954– author.
Title: Corporate strategy (remastered). I, High performance strategy and leadership in a volatile, disrupted world / Paul Hunter.
Other titles: High performance strategy and leadership in a volatile, disrupted world
Description: Abingdon, Oxon ; New York, NY : Routledge, 2020. | Includes bibliographical references and index.
Identifiers: LCCN 2020005814 (print) | LCCN 2020005815 (ebook) | ISBN 9780367253585 (hardback) | ISBN 9780429287350 (ebook)
Subjects: LCSH: Strategic planning. | Leadership.
Classification: LCC HD30.28 .H86822 2020 (print) | LCC HD30.28 (ebook) | DDC 658.4/012—dc23
LC record available at https://lccn.loc.gov/2020005814
LC ebook record available at https://lccn.loc.gov/2020005815

ISBN: 978-0-367-25358-5 (hbk)
ISBN: 978-0-429-28735-0 (ebk)

Typeset in Bembo
by Apex CoVantage, LLC

Contents

Figures

Tables

About the author

Paul Hunter is a highly experienced management consultant, educator and business executive. He is the founder and chief executive of the Strategic Management Institute, www.smi knowledge.com and a former managing director of an independent management consulting firm. Prior to establishing that entity with his colleagues, Paul was a partner with a global management consulting firm. Before entering consulting, he worked in industry in a finance and accounting capacity. He commenced the consulting stage of his career in Indonesia, where he was based for approximately two years.

A key aspect of the management consulting and education coursework presented in this book is the content developed as part of the thesis that contributed to his award of a doctor of business administration degree. Paul is a former office bearer and paper reviewer for the international Strategic Management Society. He has worked with numerous global corporations in both consulting and executive development roles. In addition to this book, he has co-authored professional practice papers and given presentations in many seminars, briefings and conferences addressing a diverse range of audiences. Examples of more recent publications and speaking engagements follow:

Publications:

The Seven Inconvenient Truths of Business Strategy, Routledge, Oxon, UK, 2014.

"Raising the Bar at Mars University": A case study and chapter in Rademakers, M. *Corporate Universities: Drivers of the Learning Organization,* Routledge, Oxon, UK, 2014.

Singapore Management Review: Co-author of "Contemporary Strategic Management Practices in Australia" and "Back to the Future, Strategy in the 2000s".

Quoted in *BRW* magazine and contributed blog posts to *Leading Company*, an online magazine.

Strategy Survey: Strategic management practice in Australian organisations in collaboration with Swinburne University.

Presentations:

Smiknowledge and Strategic Management Institute International Conference: "*Strategy as the Enabler of Change in an Era of Unbounded Disruption*", held in Melbourne in October 2017 and London November 2017. www.smiknowledge.com.

Strategy Workshops in Tehran: Appeared as the guest of the Iranian-based Strategy Academy.

Strategic Management Society: Presented in October 2017 in a conference in Houston and November 2006 in a conference in Vienna.

CPA Australia: Presentations at CPA Australia conferences, including CPA Congress in 2010 and 2013.

Chartered Institute of Management Accountants UK: Presentation in Manchester, 2017.

Institute of Directors UK: Presentation in London, 2018.

Conferences:

ANZAM: Paper presentation in 2005 titled "*The Conduct of Business Strategy in Australia*".

To contact Paul, email him at smi@smiknowledge.com, or join us on LinkedIn: www.linkedin.com/groups/3762509/. We look forward to hearing from you.

Introduction

Corporate Strategy (Remastered)

The $71 billion sale of 21st Century Fox Inc's (Fox) entertainment assets to Disney Company in 2019 marked a turning point in the career of Executive Chairman Rupert Murdoch. Finally, the hunter had become the hunted; the inventor had become the adapter. In reality, Murdoch was simply succumbing to the inevitable. Digital technology was on the rise and on the cusp of casting its shadow over the entire entertainment industry. Fox wanted out; it just didn't have the financial resources to commit to the level of investment it would need to compete with Netflix, Apple and Amazon. Disney wanted in; they did have the firepower that was needed to compete. Fox shareholders walked away with $71 billion in cash or stock options. Disney got a back-office rationalisation, additional distribution outlets and an annuity chest of classic entertainment content.

Was there any depth of strategic thinking behind Murdoch's and Disney CEO Bob Iger's decision? There undoubtedly was, and it is all on display in this book. Although neither of these two moguls may have realised it, Fox was reacting to the threat of *inertia* and charges of a failure to adapt. Disney, on the other hand, was on a fast track of *invention*, creating new opportunity (in the launch of the Disney+ television network streaming service) through a mindset we refer to as Deliberate Disruption.

> *Both Murdoch and Iger are leaders who held no fear of failure, as they were equally prepared to adapt to what is and invent what 'could be' at the same time.*

The foregoing describes some of the essential and core components that make up the remastering of conventional strategy practice. Presented within a context of Third Wave Strategy, the objective in this book is to explore, with you, methods of adaptation and invention, as well as a corporation's capacity to transform to an elevated state of high performance. Although written by a single author, Paul Hunter, it is his preference to acknowledge the work of many contributors and participants in his coursework from which this and the following *Corporate Strategy (Remastered) II* fieldbook is based. Accordingly, Paul prefers to use the terms 'we', not 'I', 'our', not 'my', and 'us', not 'me'. Some of the individuals to whom Paul owes a debt of gratitude for their contributions are Anthony Claridge, Mike Donnelly, Stuart Orr, Stephen Pitt-Walker, Gaye Mason, Greg Baker, Andrew Brown, Steve Perera, Fred Davis, Phillip Lange, Martijn Rademakers, Dianne Kelleher, Laurence Gartner, Noordin Shehabuddeen, Greg Trainor, Alexie Seller, Paul Foley, Nick Price, John Cockburn-Evans, John Toohey and Denis Bourke.

Concept of Corporate Strategy (Remastered)

In our remastering of corporate strategy, we were conscious of the fact that there was not only a need to learn about new concepts but also to unlearn old ones. In our learning, we acknowledge and applaud the initiation of formal strategy practice by Igor Ansoff (1965) through his *'lighting of the fuse'* via his groundbreaking book *Corporate Strategy*. His concepts thankfully provided a foundation upon which a remastered version of strategy could be based. In doing so, an enhanced version of the many fundamental components of strategy have been identified. An example is the integration of strategy formulation with implementation through the establishment of a systemic and fully integrated Strategic Management Framework. Another is the introduction of new dimensions of practice, both from the perspective of its structure and through extractions from cognitive and behavioural elements of the social sciences. These latter dimensions include the enactment of organisational learning; the structuring and use of deep, critical, strategic thinking; and the enablement of a culture of dialogue and engagement enacted in a context of open strategy practice.

In our unlearning, a need was recognised to disregard some of the more static and deliberate elements of the 'planning' doctrine proposed by Ansoff (1965). The world is now too unstable and complex to treat the 'doing' of strategy (strategy practice) with any degree of certainty. At the same time, the need to learn and embrace volatility, complexity and ambiguity has become an imperative if strategy practitioners are to benefit from a greater degree of freedom and boldness in their endeavours to continually disrupt, energise, transform, reinvent and renew.

How to use this book

This book is designed to act as a guide to an enhanced form of corporate strategy practice. One that incorporates, rather than hides from, the disruption created by the technological, social and economic/political transformation that represents the new order of normal that is being experienced today. Its content will appeal to any corporate leader or emerging leader seeking to enhance or pursue a successful career in business. It will provide new insight into the practice of strategy as a stand-alone document or as a component of a formal action learning or consulting program.

As a stand-alone document, it provides insight into the notion of a dynamic, system-based, structured and behaviourally conscious approach to strategy that we refer to as Third Wave Strategy. As a learning aid, the book provides groups or individuals with an understanding of ways to engage and apply the concepts associated with Third Wave Strategy and its practice. As a consulting aid, the program is presented in a facilitation mode to enable external or internal consultants, as well as other corporate strategy practitioners, to use the methodologies contained herein. Their output will be a robust company-specific strategy and ongoing capability in the management and renewal of this important aspect of management and leadership.

An overview of the structure of this book is presented in Figure 0.1. Its form and format follow a generic construct of a fully integrated Strategic Management Framework. A detailed explanation and illustration of the framework (referred to as a Third Wave Strategy framework) is presented in Chapter 1.

Ansoff's Corporate Planning legacy

The initiation of the widely recognised concept of Strategic Planning can in no small way be attributed to the unofficially anointed "father of strategy" Igor Ansoff (1965). Ansoff achieved this notoriety through the publication of his book titled *Corporate Strategy*. At the time of its writing, contemporary theories of strategy were scant and management science in general in its infancy. Preceding empirical research focused on issues of strategy and policy (Andrews, 1965) and strategy and structure (Chandler, 1962) but none focused on strategy implementation.

Ansoff was dismissive of the social sciences that addressed decision-making theory at the time of his writing. He had his reasons; he was sure that the contributions to known behavioural theories of the day were too vague to inform decision making at a strategic level. In addressing issues of a strategic nature, therefore, he thought it appropriate to follow "the tradition of the microeconomic and the behavioural theories in the sense that it is primarily concerned with the nature of the firm and not with the decision makers mind" (Ansoff, 1965). With an objective of optimising firm performance through good strategy practice, that combination he believed would help to solve what he thought was "the total strategic problem of the firm".

That problem, he supposed, was the determination of "what kind of business the firm should seek to be in". The idea of Ansoff's approach altogether was consumed with the management of four distinct 'components'. The first three were 1) the identification of potential gaps between product/market scope, 2) the realisation of opportunities presenting from 'cumulative growth vectors of new business opportunity', and 3) the opportunity to realise a competitive advantage.

The fourth was not really a component at all. It was more of a rule that stipulated that in order to meet market demand, "an organisation needed to possess an appropriate set of internal resource based synergies". The whole

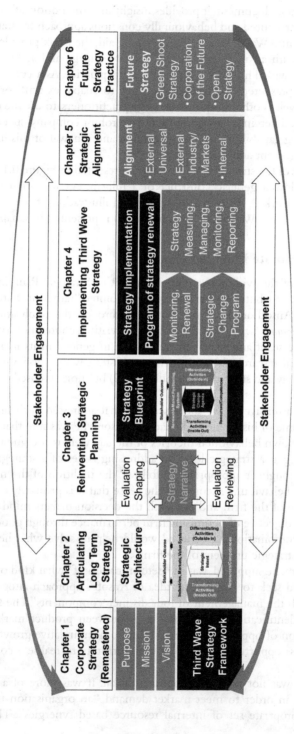

Figure 0.1 An overview of chapter structure that follows the flow of the fully integrated Strategic Management Framework used in this book

dimension of strategy was, therefore, consumed with an Outside In market-oriented growth perspective of the future. This rather obscured any notion, therefore, of an Inside Out dynamic resource base that would provide the foundation for positive change, transformation and renewal.

In the establishment of his thesis, Ansoff seems to have innocently assumed that the future could be easily predicted. Based mostly on quantitative forecasts, his strategy framework was presented as a three- to five-year strategic plan. Although he acknowledged the idea that the Corporate Plan would be affected by adverse external influences and changes in underlying assumptions, he did not deal with them in any meaningful way.

In response, our purpose in writing this book has been to explain an approach to the remastering of Ansoff's notion of static strategic or 'corporate' planning and all that has followed. Our methodology is presented in the form of a dynamic, systemic and fully integrated Strategic Management Framework. Designed as a socially aware interactive system, one that we refer to as Third Wave Strategy, our approach is driven by cognitive and behavioural aspects of the corporation's culture, management style and strength of leadership. As a dynamic system, it differentiates between strategies that are responsive to the need to continually adapt to change and the imperative to invent the type of change that will lead to the creation of 'new futures' altogether. Each are ignited by paranoia expressed in the context of continual renewal and implemented in an aura of deliberate, disruptive, positive and progressive change, transformation and renewal.

1   Concept of Corporate Strategy (Remastered)

Thematic setting: *Cognition and the operations of the fully integrated Strategic Management Framework in an era of disruption, volatility and uncertainty*

Ansoff's contribution: *Ansoff's Corporate Planning methodology addressing strategy formulation within the construct of a predictive-styled static plan prone to representation of a 'to do' list rather than a source of inspirational leadership*

Introduction: evolution of Third Wave Strategy

In writing this book, our intent was to provide insight into a dynamic way of thinking about how corporations can both survive and thrive in the new 'normal' of today's febrile business environment. This is an environment that is digesting powerful advances in technology, unconventional behaviours and an environment facing extreme threats to its sustainability. The consequences of these extremities are characterised by rapid change, dramatic disruption, extreme uncertainty, deep complexity and disarming ambiguity. In our remastering of strategy therefore, our primary task has been to

> *integrate, recalibrate and adapt known strategy practices and conceptualise, evolve, adopt and embrace fresh approaches and ideas.*

In working through the remastering exercise, we applauded, celebrated and incorporated prior empirical research. Front and centre in the field is Igor Ansoff (1965), whose seminal publication *Corporate Strategy* was born out of a new reality of optimism and prosperity. This 'feel good' environment emerged out of a long era of despair and stagnation that literally consumed the first half of the 20th century. Presented in the form of a Corporate or Strategic Plan, Ansoff's foundational work is representative of as *first wave strategy*. His contribution didn't go away, however. Far from it. Instead, many significant enhancements and additions followed, and out of the multitude of tools and techniques that were born in the 1980s, this era would see Corporate Planning evolve into a notion of Strategic Management (Schendel and Hofer, 1979). We refer to this phase of Strategic Management as *second wave strategy*. Strategy practitioners of this era enjoyed the benefits of continually evolving tools and techniques developed by academics and consultants alike. Examples are presented in Table 3.1, Chapter 3 of this book. They include assessments of industry attractiveness, models of market share analysis, product and business unit portfolio analysis, competitor analysis and more. Although many of these tools and techniques still exist today, they remain independent species that find little comfort in the sharing of a bed.

Following its rocky foundation, this 'Outside In' market-focused era wound down in the mid-1990s. At that time, a new focus on optimising efficiency and effectiveness of internal operations became a popular substitute for strategy. As an essentially 'Inside Out' management practice, the new focus was centred mostly on demands for restructuring with an emphasis on cost reduction and improvements to operating performance. Having now reached the precipice, the concept of corporate strategy in any of the foregoing formats has arrived at the brink of extinction as, arguably,

> *no new strategy practices have been identified since the arrival of the Blue Ocean Strategy (Kim & Mauborgne) in 2005.*

Further evidence of its decline abounds as

- downsizing, reengineering and outsourcing have become the new definition of strategy – even though it is known to be reactive and operational rather than proactive and strategic in nature;
- predictive analytics has become the new environmental scanning – even though it is widely accepted that the future is unpredictable;
- artificial intelligence has become the new strategic intelligence – even though it is subject to interpretation and potentially more bias than human intelligence;
- innovation has become the new strategising – even though it is unstructured and very rarely linked to perceptions or strategic visions of the future; and
- design thinking has become the new strategic thinking – even though it addresses only a minor component of strategy practice.

Where to strategy and strategy practice?

In view of the apparent enormity of change that awaits us from all perspectives of technological advances, societal norms and environmental threats, corporations can no longer afford to be complacent. Developing the means to survive and thrive will require a change in thinking, a change in outlook and a change in the way strategy is practiced.

We support, therefore, an increase in investment in organisational learning and an investment especially in ensuring professionally focused strategy practitioners are brought up to speed. The tools and constructs of the future strategy professional are described in this book and presented in a context of *Third Wave Strategy*. This form of strategy operates within the parameters of the construct of a Third Wave Strategy framework. Its operation requires the application of many human attributes that include, for example, deep (critical) thinking, an awareness of inherent bias and an appreciation of human (as well as organisational) behaviour. As our world edges closer towards a higher order of challenge and opportunity, much will be created out of further advances in the areas of digital disruption, societal change and more. It is proposed here, therefore, that a sole reliance on firm performance alone, the basis of first and second wave strategy, is problematic. Those corporate leaders who fail to change their approach to the practice of strategy, strategic leadership and strategically oriented governance will be disappointed. So much so, it must be recognised that a dogged reliance on conventional methods of strategy practice is taking corporations to a black swan moment (Taleb, 2010). This is a moment that appears suddenly and with significant force. Its arrival is usually consequential and inexplicable for those caught unwittingly in its crosshairs. It can only be dealt with in hindsight and therefore can often be irreparable. When greeted by a Black Swan moment an organisation will experience an inability to take a different approach to the conduct of strategy in practice:

> **it is literally a moment that has led many corporations to the brink of a precipitous collapse.**

A bold statement indeed, but one that is quite likely to be true, as you will witness in this book. Ultimately, it is not the lack of appreciation of strategy theory, concepts and practices that concerns us. It is more the fact that many leaders and managers find it difficult to think strategically in any structured way at all.

Corporate Strategy (Remastered) in practice: the emergence of Third Wave Strategy

In order to enhance a capacity to engage in conceptual strategic thinking, this book combines and introduces a number of strategy concepts to form our notion of Third Wave Strategy. There is little evidence of the use of this form of advanced strategy practice in large-scale organisations today. There are a few that come close, even though their actions are more likely attributable to intuition rather than informed thinking. An example of an organisation that does exhibit such attributes is the online retail company Amazon. Another is the highly renowned technology company Apple. Both are equally worthy of recognition as examples of High Performance Organisations (HPOs). Accordingly, Amazon's dramatic growth story is presented and discussed as a case study next (Case example 1.1). References to the Amazon case will be made throughout the book. The story provides insight into the thinking behind the company's founder and chief executive officer (CEO), Jeff Bezos, who intuitively or otherwise applied Third Wave Strategy concepts to practice.

Case example 1.1 Third Wave Strategy practice at Amazon

In 2018, the online store that grew from a good idea to an online global behemoth joined the likes of Apple, Berkshire Hathaway, Exxon Mobil and Walmart as a Fortune 500 top-ten lister for the first time. To get to this height, it's hard to imagine CEO Jeff Bezos and his Senior Team (S Team) sitting with a consultant around a table once a year pouring over SWOT and gap analysis as the basis for their next five-year strategic plan. Their world is far too uncertain and moving much too fast for that. What is possible is to imagine them being regularly engaged in dialogue as they challenge and goad each other on matters of critical strategic importance. Embracing complexity and thriving on uncertainty, the S Team's strategy practices are consistent with the systemic and highly advanced cognitive characteristics of Third Wave Strategy.

Principles behind Bezos's approach to strategy

Bezos must be aware of first and second wave strategy concepts but does not treat them as sacrosanct. As he seeks to deliberately break industry rules and convention in general, he treats failure as a source of learning and ignores supposed threats to Amazon's sources of competitive advantage. According to their website (Amazon, 2019), Amazon lives in a world that embraces "four core principles that guide us in delivering on our mission". They are described by Amazon as:

- *customer obsession rather than competitor focus,*
- *nurturing a passion for invention,*
- *maintaining a commitment to operational excellence, and*
- *a focus on long term thinking.*

Customer obsession rather than competitor focus

Following their interview with Bezos, Kirby and Stewart (2007) reported that it is Bezos's belief that "customer obsession is where we (Amazon) get our energy". Adopting a strategy based on customer obsession, Bezos has entrenched a culture that has allowed Amazon to become highly adept at using customer insight to "make difficult strategic decisions". Amazon's ditching of constraints imposed by normal perceptions of strategy that focus solely on the realisation of a 'competitive advantage' Bezos suggested "allows the voice of the customer to identify where and when to change, and to continually renew short term strategic plans" (Kirby and Stewart, 2007).

Amazon has emerged as a powerhouse that holds the upper hand in the fight for consumer attention over its suppliers. Accordingly, clearly defined boundaries of industries and markets don't mean much to Amazon, other than in matters of economies of scale and scope. As the owner of the direct interface between themselves and the end customer (the consumer), Amazon is extremely well placed to play suppliers one against the other. Through its subscription-only services platform, Amazon has built a loyalty program (enabled via Amazon Prime) similar to other 'regular' retailers but on steroids.

Building further on the notion of customer centricity, Bezos also sees Amazon customers as a primary source of innovation and invention. They are, Lane (2018) reported, Amazon's best informed source of insight.

Nurturing a passion for invention

As an entrepreneur and leader, Bezos has mastered the art of strategically focused invention. Operating a form of open strategy practice, it involves obtaining buy-in from all stakeholders and the formation of a senior leadership team that is open to ideas that may emerge from any level and any part of the business – at any time. Accordingly, Bezos has structured Amazon around what he calls "multiple paths to yes" (Lane, 2018). This has enabled open, strategically focused invention to be widely practiced. While it is largely perceived to be an online bookseller, Amazon carries with that the attribute of a broad-based, systems-focused capacity for strategic thinking. As an example, Amazon has been able to identify many new opportunities from its understanding and appreciation of a much broader core competency and resource base that came from just selling books. A key component of this attribute is a commitment to individual and organisational learning.

In leveraging its subscription-based loyalty program, Bezos suggests that ultimately it has become the corporation's central nervous system. It "connects everything in the company – as well as its customer base". It has in effect provided a means for Amazon to make connected expansions into new markets while also building and strengthening its core retail business (Lane, 2018). It is so central to Amazon's core that "it can't be a stand-alone business because it's completely tied into our consumer offering" (Lane, 2018). Bezos has established an entire system of connectivity in a context that we refer to as a Dynamic Market System. The notion of such a system is discussed in more detail in Chapter 2.

Maintaining a commitment to operational excellence

According to the Amazon website, "Prioritising operational performance is equivalent to prioritising the customer experience and is critical to ensuring that we maintain trust in our company". Amazon has built such an agile supply chain that all forms and types of delivery are conducted at maximum efficiency and effectiveness. The more volume they get, the larger they get. The larger they get, the more volume they can handle. The greater their volume, the more efficient they become. The greater their efficiency, the more disruptive they can be. The greater their disruption, the greater their competitive advantage or should it be said, the better their value proposition to their customers.

Consistent with the voice of Ansoff (1965), Amazon's management practices reveal a belief that if it were to be successfully disruptive, it would need to continually develop and improve its core competences – a challenge it was not afraid to embrace. Building on the core competences it already had, those of customer engagement and an excellence in retail-focused supply chain technology, Amazon has (amongst many other things), 1) become one of the world's first crowdsourcing gig marketplaces through its development of Amazon Pay, 2) sold over 100 million Echo and Dot (Alexa) gadgets since their launch and 3) evolved a technological prowess that has enabled them to become a premier supplier of cloud storage facilities, putting them on a par with Microsoft and Apple. In similar fashion to the idea of an Outside In Dynamic Market System, Bezos has also evolved an Inside Out technologically enabled Core Competence Platform, a concept also discussed in Chapter 2. The combination of each construct forms an Integrated Value System, a notion that will also be discussed in more detail in Chapter 2.

A focus on long term thinking

Amazon is no longer a start-up, so as a serious corporate player, CEO Bezos enjoys the luxury of having the time to engage in long term strategic thinking: "I very rarely get pulled into the day to day. I get to work two or three years into the future" (Lane, 2018). Complementary to a commitment to a philosophy of organisational learning, Bezos is happy to allow Amazon to invest in experiences that result in failure and then require them to ride out the after effects. So confident is he in backing failure, he reserves his regrets for experimentation on things that Amazon didn't do rather than mistakes in what they did do. He described these as "errors of omission rather than errors of commission" (Lane, 2018). They apply when a company fails to act on an apparent opportunity, even when they are capable of doing so but didn't.

Identifying new opportunity

As a strategic thinker and avid believer in organisational learning, if an opportunity arises, and Amazon doesn't have the necessary skills, Bezos will ensure a learning capability is procured to make sure that training takes place (Lane, 2018). In the evaluation of that opportunity, Amazon has established three criteria: it must be different than any other offering; it has to be big; it has to be profitable. In other words, as Carlson (2016) would suggest, they "don't sweat the small stuff".

Summation: our interpretation of Third Wave Strategy in evidence at Amazon

1   A natural appreciation of the need to take a long term perspective of company strategy, implemented cautiously with no fear of getting it wrong
2   Rapid organisational learning (fail quickly) and unlearning (habit breaking)
3   Make competition irrelevant – build a pipeline of inventions and embrace complexity
4   Focus on the design and implementation of opportunities born out of serendipity and/or deliberate invention
5   Always be on the lookout for threats requiring any form of adaptation – hold zero tolerance for inertia
6   Embrace invention – develop a systems approach to the design and construct of product and service solutions
7   Follow a relentless pursuit of organic growth delivered through continual adoption of specific programs of organisational transformation and regeneration
8   Base the desire for organic growth on the physical, technological and/or 'virtual' platform upon which all core and new business is conducted and evolved
9   Adopt an open approach to organisational development and strategy at a corporate level as used

   •   by the formal strategising group: the S Team;
   •   by users of other team-based challenges, looking to break down dominant mental models;
   •   through the practice of open innovation and strategy practice at all levels of the business.

10   Turn learning into knowledge as a contributor to strategically focused augmented intelligence: enabled through deep, critical thinking and in-depth data analytics
11   Ensure alignment – especially between strategy, structure, systems and operations
12   Enhance high performance leadership capabilities: achieving extraordinary results through the empowerment of ordinary people.

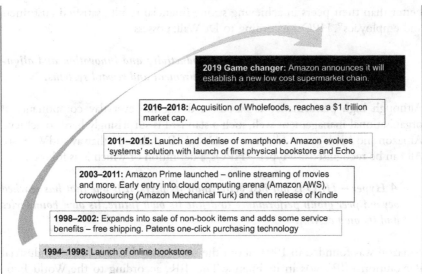

2019 Game changer: Amazon announces it will establish a new low cost supermarket chain.

2016–2018: Acquisition of Wholefoods, reaches a $1 trillion market cap.

2011–2015: Launch and demise of smartphone. Amazon evolves 'systems' solution with launch of first physical bookstore and Echo

2003–2011: Amazon Prime launched – online streaming of movies and more. Early entry into cloud computing arena (Amazon AWS), crowdsourcing (Amazon Mechanical Turk) and then release of Kindle

1998–2002: Expands into sale of non-book items and adds some service benefits – free shipping. Patents one-click purchasing technology

1994–1998: Launch of online bookstore

Figure 1.1 A brief history of Amazon

An illustration of the growth of Amazon from its launch in 1994 through today appears as Figure 1.1.

By 2010, more people bought ebooks than physical books from Amazon.com. By 2017, it became only the second trillion dollar company in the world. In his 2017 letter to Amazon's shareholders, Bezos warned of stagnation, which he suggested was similar to a state of inertia. Having started with a modest ambition of selling books online, Bezos's implied organisational purpose for Amazon was to be 'the everything store'. Now however,

> *Bezos has consciously or otherwise broadened Amazon's organisational purpose, from that of 'the everything store' to one of 'the platform for the everything store'.*

Neither Bezos nor Amazon fear any constraints in their ambition, capability and capacity for growth.

Dimensions of Third Wave Strategy: bringing strategy back from the brink

In describing the concept of Third Wave Strategy, the characteristics of an HPO are identified as a point of reference. Insight into the notion of an HPO is provided by de Wall (2010), who described such an entity as "those that are better than their peers in achieving strong financial results, satisfied customers and employees". HPOs, according to De Wall, possess

> *high levels of individual initiative, productivity and innovation and alignment to appropriate performance measurement and reward systems.*

Although high performance is based on doing the everyday components of organisational management well, such a standard is surprisingly hard to achieve. Amazon and Apple are standouts, as are Google, Berkshire Hathaway and Walmart. All can be recognised as Hyper – HPOs, a definition of which is as follows:

> *A Hyper – HPO is not just better than its peers; it is one that has reached beyond peer group performance to define its own future, its own boundaries and its own destiny.*

Amazon was founded in 1994, about the same time that the Fourth Industrial Revolution (4IR) was in its infancy. The 4IR, according to the World Economic Forum website,

> "represents a new chapter in human development, enabled by technology advances that are commensurate with those of the first, second and third industrial revolutions, and which are merging the physical, digital and biological worlds in ways that create both promise and peril. The speed, breadth and depth of this revolution is forcing us to rethink how countries should develop, how organizations create value, and even what it means to be human".

At the time of its incorporation, competitors saw Amazon as a minnow that would never be a threat to the incumbent giants of the in-store book retailing industry, such as Barnes and Noble and Waterstones. Both doubled down on their efforts to persevere with the survival of the traditional bookshop retail store for a long time after online shopping became available. Just as the fortunes of these stores declined, however, Amazon's rose.

Third Wave Strategy as practice: things that Third Wave Strategy practitioners do

A late development from the era of second wave strategy has been the recognition that the physical 'doing' of strategy is a much-needed antidote to the shortcomings of conventional strategic management, which is now largely seen as something a firm 'has'. Examples of 'have' are described by Whittington and Calluit (2018) as being similar "to an organisational property". Students of strategy theory will be familiar with these examples, they include "multivariate analyses of firm performance" and "vertical integration and the scope of the firm".

In contrast, a notion of strategy practice as something a firm *does*, is described by Jarzabkowski and Spee (2009) as a lived experience prosecuted by:

i **Practitioners:** those who do the work of strategy
ii **Practices:** the social, symbolic and material tools through which strategy is done, and
iii **Praxis:** the flow of activity through which strategy is accomplished.

This insight provides us with a useful construct within which Third Wave Strategy concepts can be readily explored. Our exploration commences with a review of the players – the practitioners who carry out the act of strategy practice.

Practitioners: those who do Third Wave Strategy

Prior to the formalisation of Corporate Planning, strategy was largely an instruction issued by the head office. Its practice was often referred to as strategy and policy rather than strategy *per se*. Seen largely as an elitist corporate activity, current trends consistent with a Third Wave Strategy philosophy are breaking down many of the barriers created by such elitism. Increasingly, the conduct of strategy is moving towards an open program – a format identified previously as a feature of Amazon's management practices (Case example 1.1). In place of the select few, open strategy invites, acknowledges and responds to the views and opinions of a broad range of stakeholders in the business.

That doesn't mean that the senior leadership doesn't have any input anymore. It does mean that the organisation benefits from a range of sources of insight, foresight and hindsight delivered via a broad range of stakeholders. In effect, open strategy enables the etching out of useful factual data developed by the formal strategy practitioners and those of authority who are really 'in the know' in terms of strategic issues impacting the firm. It also captures the intuitive, speculative and grounded knowledge of those who have traditionally had very little access to the leadership. This often ignored source of knowledge can be precious; it consists of individuals who are found in close proximity to the heart and soul of the company. They include shop floor employees and those engaged directly with the customers and other stakeholders.

Legitimising the role of the corporate strategy practitioner

As someone reading this book, you will no doubt be extremely interested in, or closely associated with, the skills required to be a strong strategy practitioner. As you read, you will find that the practice of Third Wave Strategy will strengthen your skills in this important field. In the absence of a workable framework, good practitioners have long relied on intuition and 'gut feel' as a source of inspiration and strategic decision making. Research conducted by Ohmae (1982) on this matter is conclusive. Through his research into the secrets of successful CEOs in Japan, Ohmae discovered that those who could think like a 'strategist' were individuals who "intuitively possess a basic grasp of the fundamental elements of strategy".

Regrettably only a few possess such powers. In his book *Good Strategy, Bad Strategy*, Rumelt (2011) observed that the practice of good strategy can be quite difficult for many. Engineers, for example, "expect to design and build a bridge that lasts". They are "conflicted by the idea that strategy cannot be as concise as a bridge design".

> ***This strategy stuff is vacuous one engineer complained. We need to know what our options are and then pick the best solution.***

Recognising that engineers do indeed build bridges based on certainty and a guarantee that they won't fall down, Rumelt needed to find a way to explain the nature and extent of uncertainty in strategy. He concluded that as a social science, "strategy is like a hypothesis" – that is, "an educated guess about what will work, not a wild theory, but an educated judgement". Rumelt (2011) surmised that when viewing strategy in this context, practitioners must reframe their thinking by breaking away from preconceived mental models of 'what is' and instead remain open to the idea of uncertainty and ambiguity. At the same time, they should also feel comfortable with rigour and complexity. Similar to intuition, comfort factors that offset uncertainty and ambiguity are often an absent component of corporate life. A key reason for that is the fact that there has not been a suitable Strategic Management Framework that brings all of the components of strategy theory and practice together – until now.

In addition to the Third Wave Strategy framework upon which strategy can be effectively structured, it is also apparent that the source of knowledge proposed by Rumelt is derived from learning, at both a personal and organisational level. It was also Senge's (1990) observation that systems thinking, personal mastery and breaking of mental models are key to organisational learning. From our perspective, organisational learning lies at the heart of good strategy. Helping us to "learn within the unknowable" (Flood, 1999), Senge (1990) has proposed that systems thinking provides the ideal platform for organisational learning. Systems thinking is Senge implies, the holy grail of organisational learning, a strength of corporate development and great strategy practice.

Institutionalisation vs. open, Third Wave Strategy: The conduct and capture of Third Wave Strategic thinking

It is difficult to institutionalise different perspectives of strategic thinking in any one corporation or individual for that matter. In many ways, the inherent constrictions naturally associated with the concept of institutionalisation in any form are an anathema to the boundaryless oriented, disruptive and systems-focused attributes of the more advanced forms of Third Wave Strategy. The value of such an attribute is perhaps one reason why there is increasingly a strong orientation towards the notion of open strategy practice over that of rote form filling. The adoption of either approach will always depend on the prevailing nature of a corporation's leadership style and culture.

Some organisations do institutionalise a method of strategy practice and strategic thinking. They include Toyota with its Toyota Way, GE with the GE Way and in a time gone by, Hewlett Packard (HP) with its HP Way. Each delivered significant benefits to their respective organisations. Toyota still does enjoy those benefits. Practitioners of the Toyota Way suggested, in fact, that it encourages open strategic thinking and the realisation of the benefits of innovation. The question is, are they capable of supporting notions of Third Wave Strategy?

It is our belief that they do, but it is not a mandatory requirement for good strategy practice. As long as they adopt the same form of institutionalisation demonstrated by Toyota, for example, it should work well. Consistent with open strategy practice, the Toyota Way is grounded in a philosophy of dialogue, engagement and openness. In every instance and with everything strategy, however, neither institutionalisation, open strategy nor anything in between should be taken for granted, and nothing should be taken literally. That really is the nature of strategy, as will be observed time and time again throughout this book. Our observation? Strategy is riddled with uncertainty, complexity and ambiguity.

Although the future is open to all of us to craft, it can't be done with any degree of certainty, simplicity or guaranteed clarity.

Third Wave Strategy practice: the social, symbolic and material tools through which Third Wave Strategy is done

The notion of Third Wave Strategy is grounded in the observation that

in a world of increasing uncertainty, complexity and ambiguity, it is no longer acceptable for leaders to sit back and hope to adapt to 'what is'.

Instead, leaders and strategy practitioners must be both

* resilient in their maintenance of, and commitment to, a continual adaptation to 'what is' and what 'might be' and
* aggressive in the pursuit, evaluation, invention, selection and implementation of multiple alternatives of what 'could be'.

Each option requires corporate leaders of established organisations, especially to embrace a notion of explorative, multi-opportunity seeking.

To maintain resilience *and* engage in multidextrous research, Hyper – HPOs must be prepared to

- constantly monitor the prevailing business environment and
- identify, initiate and lead explorations into the identification of future opportunity.

To do both is to exercise a rite of passage to a new world order – one typically characterised today by disruptive technology, social enlightenment and ecological reformation. That level of transformation essentially requires a remastering of the way of *doing* strategy. A recognition and explanation of the extent and type of change required lies behind the concept of Third Wave Strategy, which supposes that

> *to survive, an organisation needs to be able to adapt to 'what is', to thrive a corporation must be dynamic in the realisation of a choice between multiple alternatives of what 'could be'.*

Put simply, an organisation must be equally prepared to adapt to change as much as it is to invent it. It is our recommendation, therefore, that practitioners embrace a perspective of strategic thinking that introduces the idea of recognising and exploiting the notions of both adaptation and invention:

- Adaptation is concerned with the management of responses to anticipated and unanticipated change.
- Invention is concerned with the deliberate design and creation of one or multiple new futures that in many cases will be created through deliberately disruptive means.

> *The process of adaptation can be described as a reactive or proactive <u>response</u> to change that can be seen or expected. Equally, the use of the term <u>prosponse</u> can be used to describe as an appropriate reference to a reactive or proactive invention that points practitioners towards an envisaged future that is yet to be fulfilled.*

In the absence of a clear appreciation of the relationship between re and prosponse, each are explained as follows:

- **Response:** Adaptive strategic change adopted by an organisation provoked into an action that is the outcome of an expected or unexpected external or internal stimulus that occurs beyond the organisations control, thereby initiating programs of survival.
- **Prosponse:** An invented strategic change introduced on terms that are within the organisations control and evoked as a result of a deliberate intent to positively challenge or disrupt that organisation's future strategic trajectory, thereby initiating programs of thrival.

Most corporations consistently practice only one of these forms of strategic change, which we describe as a state of sponse. A definition of sponse is as follows:

A knowledge-driven state of change that is provoked or evoked as an outcome from a change in the organisation's circumstances or as a result of the identification of new opportunity that has become apparent within a system's internal and/or external environment.

To add clarity, we illustrate four different perspectives of sponse in the matrix shown in Figure 1.2. Here you will observe an interpretation and description of the environment within which various companies in the retail supermarket industry can be recognised for their states of 'sponsiveness' with regard to degrees of reactive and proactive behaviour.

Content described in the sponse matrix demonstrates the nature of strategic change and by association the state of strategic thinking that could be experienced by supermarket retail chains depicted therein. As a general rule, the more prosponsive the chain, the more disruptive and inventive it is. Supermarket chains residing in a state of Inertia (Quadrant 1) exercise low or no levels of prosponsiveness. Occupants here will be wallowing in an apparent state of stagnation or decline. Characterised by static or no growth, hopes for success are nailed to perceptions of a 'lowest cost' form of competitive advantage. This has a knock-on effect though as the quality of products sold and services provided also diminish at the same or an even greater rate. Regrettably, when

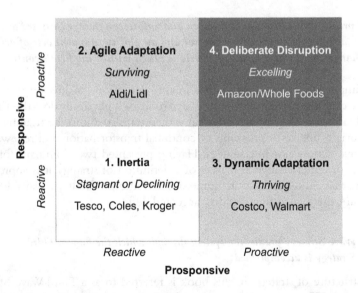

Figure 1.2 Matrix of sponsive strategic change

cost and quality are reflected in selling price alone, any business's value proposition is automatically reduced to the status of a commodity where price is the only thing that matters. As discussed in Chapter 4, competition amongst commodity providers is fraught and likely to end in a "vicious cycle of value destruction". Supermarket chains referred to in Quadrant 2 and 3 demonstrate a degree of survivability, but the greater the absence of prosponsiveness, the more difficult it will be to thrive. The examples presented in Quadrant 2, Aldi and Lidle, are Agile Adapters that have redefined low-cost supermarket retailing but have not reinvented it. An example of a supermarket chain that is a Dynamic Adapter is Costco (Quadrant 3). This chain has designed a membership-based platform and value proposition that allows it to maintain a close relationship with its customer base. In this way, it has evolved a higher level of value to its customers. Although more expensive to operate, it offsets a loss of margin from high volume individual sales by winning a greater share of wallet via higher sales volume per customer. In the final corner (Quadrant 4), the ultimate winner is unsurprisingly Amazon and its recent acquisition, Whole Foods. Through the enactment of Deliberate Disruption, Amazon is in good company with organisations that enjoy a life of continual reinvention and renewal.

Definition of strategy

Armed with an appreciation of the concept of sponse, it is now possible to establish a conclusive definition of strategy of relevance to a Third Wave Strategy environment. Strategy is

> *a preparedness to adapt to foreseen and unforeseen change initiated as a result of factors beyond the firm's control and an ability to invent acts of deliberate change created as a result of decisions taken within the firm's control.*

It is important to understand that in this definition, positive organisational change can be seen as the key objective of strategy. It physically does this through the identification of opportunity that is then translated into the trialling and, if appropriate, uptake of programs of continual transformation and renewal – of the organisation, not just strategy. Having presented two dominant forms of growth-oriented change as drivers of a definition of strategy, it is appropriate to note that although there are numerous definitions of strategy available in the literature, there is no single widely accepted definition.

Third Wave Strategy praxis: the system through which the flow of Third Wave Strategy is accomplished

The structure of strategy in this book is referred to as a Third Wave Strategy framework. When treated as a system, this framework goes a long way towards providing an appropriate form and format within which all dimensions of strategy theory and practice can find a common language, context, format and structure. It is fair to say, therefore, that

> *the Third Wave Strategy framework presented in this book provides an ideal platform upon which strategy practitioners can structure their thinking, strengthen their leadership skills and raise the effectiveness of strategy practice overall.*

This philosophy and description of the use of an integrated framework is given extra weight by HPO specialist de Waal (2010), who suggested,

> *An integrated approach to strategic management is a key feature of a firm's capacity to reach levels of high performance.*

As another example of consistency between the framework, high performance and, indeed, the notion of open strategy practice, de Vaal also observed what can be considered to be the very essence of Third Wave Strategy:

> *HPO's management processes are integrated with the strategy, structure, processes and people who are aligned throughout the organisation.*

Fundamental to the practice of strategy generally is the observation that because it is impossible to accurately predict the future, it is highly likely that strategy practitioners will get things wrong. It should be readily accepted therefore, that this will create annoyance and disappointment, especially in the form of unintended consequences. Strategy practitioners therefore must be afforded forgiveness, when engaging in the act of strategic thinking. An exception though is the circumstance where practitioners have failed to test the assumptions and estimations that form the basis of their strategic decisions. In order to avoid this occurrence, it is appropriate that those factors of uncertainty are reviewed and renewed on an ongoing basis. That is just one more reason why there is a compelling need to remaster the practice of corporate strategy overall.

Third Wave Strategy framework

A high-level representation of the design of a fully integrated Third Wave Strategy framework appears as Figure 1.3. Fundamental to its operation is the capability to maintain relevance, consistency, renewal and alignment. The Third Wave Strategy framework provides a platform for strategic decision making.

> *Embedded in a philosophy of continual strategy renewal, it provides a viable, comprehensive, expanded and integrated alternative to Ansoff's model of Corporate Planning.*

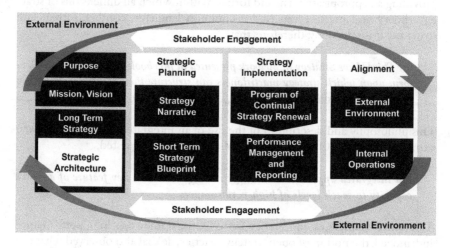

Figure 1.3 High-level strategy system and foundation of a Third Wave Strategy framework

Construct and management of the Third Wave Strategy framework

As a systems-based approach to strategy practice,

> **the Third Wave Strategy framework is of equal relevance to disruptive plotters as it is to mechanistic planners.**

The idea of a framework is consistent with Ansoff's (1965) basic design of a Corporate Plan. Unlike Ansoff's model, however, the Third Wave Strategy framework incorporates and integrates practices of strategy formulation and implementation. From an operations perspective, it demands an appreciation of the nuances of human behaviour, bias and the science of cognition while not ignoring the need for a focus on firm performance.

> **Based on a philosophy that embraces complexity and an immunity to the fear of failure, the Third Wave Strategy framework provides the mechanism within which deep, critical thinking and a passion for organisational learning can thrive.**

The framework operates as a mechanism that is supportive of, but not limited to, design oriented, innovative and open strategy practice. These actions are invigorated and renewed through a focus on *re* and *pro*sponsive strategic thinking (Figure 1.2). Similarly, an appreciation of organisational Purpose, a consciousness of Mission and an inspirational Vision each provide a solid grounding for the formation and implementation of strategy.

In its entirety, the integrated design of the framework for the first time ensures a seamless link between purpose, vision, formulation, evaluation, implementation and operations.

Individual elements of the framework

As a key component of element 1 of the Third Wave Strategy framework, Long Term Strategy is presented in the construct of a Strategic Architecture. The second element of the framework, Strategic Planning, is representative of a reinvention of Ansoff's Corporate Planning methodology. Our objective here, however, is to replace the notion of a static, annual and ritualistic Corporate Plan with a document that we refer to as a Strategy Narrative.

A Strategy Narrative assumes a format of an ongoing virtual discourse rather than a static documented 'to do' list. Content includes details of the reasoning, assumptions and expectations behind the Short Term Strategy, an identification of strategic objectives, as well as intended outcomes. A structure that encapsulates the output from a Strategy Narrative is that of a Strategy Blueprint. The Strategy Blueprint is the feeder to actions articulated in, and slated for Strategy Implementation.

Illustrated as the third element of the framework, Strategy Implementation is conducted within a formal Program of Continual Strategy Renewal. In this context, strategy practitioners can be assured that strategy will always retain its relevance and its value. The fourth element of the strategy framework, Alignment (and often realignment) reflects the need for all components of the framework to act in harmony within, without and beyond the Third Wave Strategy system.

Why a framework?

In establishing a platform for strategy, it is useful to borrow from Bolman and Deal (2017) to demonstrate how a frame (or framework) can be used. A frame, they suggest, is representative of a valuable tool upon which a mental model can be readily recalled and imagined in our minds. This frame is then redeployed when the need arises, enabling all stakeholders to read, understand and negotiate a new 'territory' within the frame.

A model of strategy expressed as a framework provides a capacity to understand and imagine how each of the different tools and techniques located within the system can be used – where, when and why. The better the model, Bolman and Deal suggested, the easier it is to know where you are and how to get around. Not only does it help us to know when to use scenario planning or market share analysis, for example, it also provides practitioners with an idea of where they should go next and what they should do when they get there. Another advantage of the framework is its foundation as a common language upon which strategy can be readily discussed, reviewed, renewed and simulated.

Third Wave Strategy in a nutshell

In this chapter, many aspects of Third Wave Strategy are introduced. A summary of a generic version of its content appears as Figure 1.4. Based on a definition of strategy that has *re* and *pro*sponsive strategic change as its key driver, Third Wave Strategy consists of up to eight key elements. In reality, there may be more or fewer elements than those presented here. The actual number will depend on the unique circumstances of each corporate entity.

Summing up

In the ensuing chapters of this book details of each of the four primary elements of the Third Wave Strategy framework are explored further. By way of introduction to the detail contained in the framework a more comprehensive version is presented in Figure 1.5.

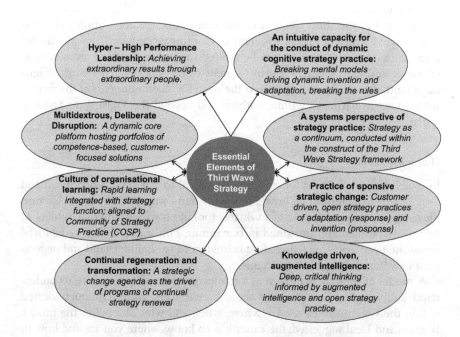

Figure 1.4 Generic version of the eight essential elements of Third Wave Strategy

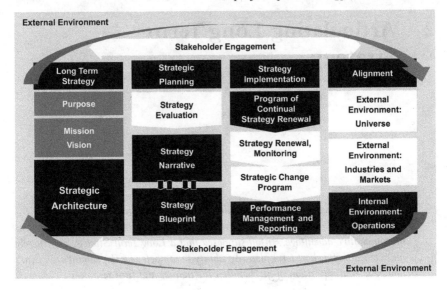

Figure 1.5 Expanded depiction of the Third Wave Strategy framework

As suggested in our introduction, the framework provides the basis for the structuring of each chapter of this book and the companion fieldbook, *Corporate Strategy (Remastered) II.*

2 Articulating Long Term Strategy

Thematic setting: *Strategic positioning and strategising for the long term*
Ansoff's contribution: *With a focus on Short Term Strategy and an emphasis on competitive advantage, Ansoff supposed that a Long Term Strategy was merely an extension of a short term plan. An ability to compete was dependant on a firm's ability to find a position of 'fit' between the market and firm resources*

Introduction: contextualising the evolution of Long Term Strategy practice

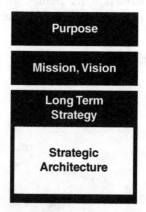

In this chapter, we take a tour of the first element of the Third Wave Strategy framework, that of Long Term Strategy. The tour commences with Purpose, Mission, Vision and follows with a review of the implications of Long Term Strategy on the business. This is followed with an exploration of the construct that was developed to represent Long Term Strategy: the Strategic Architecture.

The components of Purpose, Mission, Vision, we note, are only expressions of a hypothesis unless they are extrapolated into an articulation of strategy. In taking a long term perspective, you are invited to consider what Long Term Strategy is and isn't.

To set the scene, imagine the nervous energy that is generated when the strategy and leadership team meets to conduct a formal one- to two-day strategic planning 'retreat' or 'offsite'. Both the nature of the event and its name are symbolic representations of a tribal ceremony. Centre stage is the fast-track MBA graduate whose burning ambition is to become the tribal chief – or CEO. This person has been asked to organise the planning event and put the subsequent outcomes together as a strategic plan. The chalice she is given, however, is nearly always a poisoned one. The workshop she has been asked to convene is meant to develop a short term strategic plan, not a Long Term Strategy. It is not her fault that she has no idea what the difference is between the two, none of her colleagues recognise the difference either. In making the mistake, she is simply highlighting the fact that there is a lot of confusion about what strategy is in general.

Ansoff (1965) also failed to differentiate between Long and Short Term Strategy in any meaningful way. In his mind, he simply thought of the long term as an extension of a short term forecast-based strategic plan. To clarify, both are separate but related; however, broadly speaking,

a strategic plan is a description of the way that Long Term Strategy will be implemented – in the short term.

As often happens in practice today, the innocent strategy workshop convener who has spent some time in the accounting or similar administration department could well see the planning process as something like a two- to three-year extension of the one-year budget. That is because they will probably be relying on prevailing company-specific traditions, forms and frameworks used in past years. Alternatively, they may be relying on the views expressed in the textbook they used at business school. Inevitably, the focus of the planning event will be placed very much on the development (often from scratch) of many of the issues that should more appropriately be concerned with Long Term Strategy but are not. Similarly, many long term issues are confused with Short Term Strategy, making short term initiatives hard to identify and even harder to implement.

A consequential outcome from not differentiating between the two is the apparent overemphasis on short term thinking in business at the expense of long term strategising. As an example of how this difference in emphasis plays out, Hamel and Prahald (1994), made an astonishing accusation in the *Harvard Business Review* that is still relevant today: "Most layoffs at large US companies have been the fault of managers who fell asleep at the wheel and missed the turnoff for the future". It's fair to say that if the future is only defined by the next three, even five years, it is no wonder that these executives overlooked the need to invest in new capital or redirect existing capital in 10- to 20-year cycles. It is also no wonder that strategies of operationally focused adaptation (cost reduction, reengineering and outsourcing) overshadowed the far more growth-oriented strategies of prosponsive invention and everything else that goes with a 10- to 50-year outlook (as will be observed in the Ford Case example 2.3).

Nor is it any wonder that

> *a compulsion to focus on short term strategic planning has left long standing industry incumbents wallowing in a state of despair as agile, future focused start-ups disrupt entire industries.*

The truth is, such start-ups are unencumbered by ageing, high-cost plants and equipment and old-fashioned financing methods. So are they unencumbered by ageing, high-cost thinking and old-fashioned leadership styles. With a focus on the long term, they are free to deploy lower-cost, agile infrastructures funded by financial mechanisms that didn't exist even a short time ago. They are, therefore, able to literally knock industry incumbents off their perch, one by one.

Isn't that the point though?

> *Why is it that mature, well-resourced organisations are continuously being outgunned by those with much less experience, much more debt and much higher risk?*

This question becomes more purposeful when it is realised that much of what has been discussed in this chapter is of relevance to business unit strategy rather than corporate level strategy. Even then the question that should be asked is, "Aren't smaller-sized business units capable of being just as agile as start-ups?" Perhaps the difference stems from the fact that it is only the strategy practitioners in the head office who have the luxury of looking a long way into the future? Our answer lies in our observation that

> *while corporate level strategy is focused on business unit and financial portfolios, insufficient attention is being given to business unit–specific customer service and product portfolios.*

With only a three- to five-year outlook, business unit leaders are bound to overemphasise adaptation over invention, restructuring over transforming and cost reduction over resource optimisation. It's not that they were 'falling asleep at the wheel', it was just that their priorities lie elsewhere.

Corporate Strategy (Remastered) in practice: Long Term, Third Wave Strategy and the Strategic Architecture

In seeking to redirect business unit priorities back to the management of, and differentiation between, Long and Short Term Strategies, it is appropriate to ask the question: Why do it? In seeking an answer, Porter (2008) observed that the practice of strategy is a fundamental component of leadership:

> *For any organisation, developing a strategy is an act of leadership, and strategy represents perhaps the most powerful tool available to leaders to get all*

the individuals in the organisation aligned around a common sense of purpose and direction.

It is also an essential skill and part of Hyper – HPO leadership. At some point, however, everyone in a corporation will be called upon to think strategically. In presenting another reason to do strategy, Amazon (Case example 1.1) again provides insight. Here, CEO Jeff Bezos's definition of organisational purpose has, conceptually at least, evolved from becoming 'the everything store' to "the platform for the everything store". Even as a notional illustration of an organisation's continual transformation, it reflects the very essence of what Amazon is about:

> *As a result of the strength of Bezos's underlying strategy, Amazon was able to emerge from its roots as a simplistic, online bookstore to that of an industry sized technological giant.*

The Amazon giant participates in global industries and markets and a network of services and product solutions and it is a leader in software and hardware technology. This is reason enough to 'do' strategy, isnt it?.

The Amazon story, however, stands in stark contrast to another retailer that, ironically, has its roots in a similarly styled supply chain that Amazon has today. That retailer is Sears Holdings – an organisation that arguably found it difficult to differentiate between Short and Long Term Strategy as well as strategy and operations. The difference in performance between Amazon and Sears is stark, as demonstrated in Case example 2.1.

Case example 2.1   Long Term Strategy at Sears retail

In business, there is rarely a well-understood articulation of Long Term Strategy. Sometimes, but only rarely, there is no strategy at all. Regrettably, no strategy can be better than bad strategy. Take the US retail giant Sears as an example. Established in the late 1800s, Sears was the first retailer to enter the remote order and home delivery business. Instead of the online ordering and courier delivery service deployed by online retailers today, Sears operated a catalogue publication and mail ordering system.

Remaining true to its long term objectives, Sears was both willing and able to adapt to a rapidly changing world. As its core customer base gradually migrated from country to city, so too did Sears transform from a virtual long distance distributor to a brick and mortar retailer. Just like every other retailer in the world, the market for household products matured in the late 1990s. Sears wasn't alone though as it was forced by the arrival of online shopping to seek opportunities to rationalise its resource base and etch out alternative sources of revenue to its traditional retail outlets. In order to fulfil its objectives and, realistically, its survival, Sears merged with another retailer, Kmart, and a range of other related businesses.

Although Sears's reliance on catalogue sales was largely diminished by the turn of the century, Sears's archives suggest they reactivated that form of selling in some way in the mid-2000s. The rational was clear if you read the chairman's letter to shareholders in February 2011. It provided them with a foundational platform for customer engagement and all the benefits that come with that.

With these foundations in place, transformation to a brave new (online) world should have been a breeze. It wasn't. Rather than adopting a plan of transformation supported by a newly minted form of supply chain and an analytics capability of distinction, Sears instead chose to invest borrowed cash in online retailing but not in the format that most retailers have adopted. Long term investor and now CEO Eddie Lampert explained Sears's strategy in a company blog posting in September 2018: "The Company has been working hard to transform to a member-centric company". This, he suggested, was one that sought to integrate its physical store network, its service businesses and its Shop Your Way membership program.

Hoping to emulate Amazon in the establishment of a construct that we refer to as a Core Competence Platform, the Shop Your Way initiative was in reality nothing more than a regular member rewards program. Essentially, its capability was limited to the means to allow frequent buyers to accumulate points for their Sears and Kmart purchases and then turn them into coupon and discount equivalents. It is reported that the primary goal of Shop Your Way (Peterson, 2017) was to acquire customers' personal information and sell it to other companies. This knowledge, however, would have been of little help in growing Sears's business. It was still a long way away from being anything like the online retailing company that took Amazon to success.

Facing a downhill spiral towards bankruptcy, Chairman Lampert remained committed to the business throughout. In his February 2016 report to shareholders he wrote, "We believe that our investments in the membership platform and our integrated retail capabilities were more appropriate investments given the massive shift in how customers are shopping and how competition has evolved". Sears, though, had neglected its increasingly dilapidated portfolio of retail outlets according to Peterson (2017). Forsaking a dire need to invest in store maintenance, Sears instead hung its hat on a transformation to something it couldn't achieve – a cashed-up resource base, a business generating free cash flow and the right level and mix of people with skills sufficient to satisfy the vision of its newly defined business platform. For Lampert, it seems the ambition was far greater than the reality. Under a purported shaky leadership style (Peterson, 2017), Sears inevitably missed the opportunity to successfully transform to a combined online *and* bricks-and-mortar powerhouse *supported by* (as opposed to *transforming to*) a member-centric customer loyalty program. As a result, Sears was forced to continually stave off Chapter 11 bankruptcy.

Unusually, it seems the Sears experience is the opposite of the normal situation, as the transformation journey designed by Sears was based on the implementation of long term objectives that passed for a Short Term Strategy. In the absence of a well-understood and accepted Short Term Strategy, cracks appeared everywhere. The long term objectives didn't have a chance of succeeding in the short term. Sears perilously excluded the essential maintenance of the physical stores and the management of other more mundane essentials of business. At the end of the day, the transformation was mostly about financial restructuring and little about a well-thought-through program of emergent organisational renewal. The concept of organisational transformation and renewal will be explored in more detail in Chapter 4.

An assessment of the elements of Long Term Strategy

As shown in Figure 1.5, Long Term Strategy is made up of two primary components: 1) Purpose, Mission, Vision and 2) the construct of a Strategic Architecture. Each of these elements are discussed next.

Organisational Purpose, Mission, Vision: the foundation of Long Term Strategy

While it was possible to demonstrate Amazon's very strong commitment to an expression of Purpose, it is difficult to find a similar statement at Sears. An imperative for a corporation to develop and live by a statement of organisational purpose is the outcome from extensive research conducted by Mayer (2018) on behalf of the British Academy. Mayer defines Purpose as

> *the reason a corporation is created and exists, what it seeks to do and what it seeks to become.*

It is quite noticeable from this definition that the reasoning supporting a statement of purpose is considerably different that those of Mission and Vision. A corporate mission is described by De Wit and Meyer (2010) as "an enduring set of principles that provide guidance to strategy practitioners as they consciously reflect on, or question, organisational purpose". When engaged in the process of making strategic choices, De Wit and Meyer suggest that the set of principles should include

- an articulation of the beliefs upon which the corporate vision can be grounded;
- a description of the values that its stakeholders must acknowledge, respect and adhere to; and
- a broad-based explanation of what the company is about.

A Vision on the other hand describes an ambition, a motivational description of fundamental beliefs and an expression of what it "dreams of achieving". An example is "to be the leading provider of garden tools in the world". At its lowest level, a Vision provides direction upon which a Purpose and Mission can be grounded. At a higher level, a Vision provides the opportunity for the leadership team to create an atmosphere that inspires, motivates and energises others. At an even higher level, it is the lifeblood upon which those on the leadership team and board of directors can express and share their passion for an envisioned future of the business they lead.

> *A vision is a lived and shared experience and the basis upon which the leadership of a business is collectively motivated to take their company to ever higher levels of performance.*

Imagine, for example, if the vison developed by the founder of company that wants to be "the leading provider of garden tools in the world" was in fact expressed by a high school graduate working out of the garage at his parent's house. This exhibits great (long term) ambition but not a reason for an organisation to exist (Purpose) or an "enduring set of principles" that makes up a Mission. Both Mission and Vision inform and motivate the practice of strategy but are not the reason it is done. What strategy does do is provide the means for an organisation to identify, manifest, renew and continually align everything it does with its intended Purpose. It is fair to conclude, therefore, that the key reason to invest in the 'doing' of strategy is to satisfy its Purpose.

Content of Long Term Strategy

In an articulation of Long Term Strategy, it could be expressed as

> *a description of the Strategic Imperatives that an organisation must have or do if it is to deliver a firm's Purpose, desired outcomes and results – in the long term.*

Examples of expressions of a Strategic Imperative are: "a technologically advanced and integrated operating platform, a culture of trust and values, a policy of continual renewal and a capability in organisational learning". Strategic

Imperatives are unlikely to change very much over time. In today's business environment, however, the impact of change is arguably significantly greater than in Ansoff's era, for example. Ultimately, therefore, degrees of change will vary from one stage of economic stability to another and from one company to another. In a world of emerging digitalisation and disruption, the firm really has only two options available to it if it is to both survive and thrive. As suggested previously, they are the *re-* and *pro*sponsive actions that form the sponse matrix illustrated in Figure 1.2. These actions will in turn be influenced largely by forces that are as follows:

- **Outside In in perspective:** Those forces imposed on the firm from the external environment within which it competes
- **Inside Out in perspective:** The forces arising from actions taken within the firm in its efforts to exert its own influences on itself and the external environment

Strategic environment for Long Term, Third Wave Strategy: influence of external and internal forces

It has been a long-held belief that external influences originating from Outside In industry dynamics and other phenomenon in the external environment will have the potential to limit the scope of a firm's strategic ambitions. This is an often disputed observation in empirical research. Our own research found that 82% of senior executives agreed that their strategy is dictated "primarily by industry forces and emerging trends". From a practical perspective, therefore, it is apparent that

true or not, there is some belief that strategy is influenced by random external forces, and such a perception should be managed accordingly.

What this means, is that strategy practitioners should always seek to address the potential for external influences on firm-specific strategy. Certainly, an ingrained philosophy of limiting ambition to industry-specific opportunity has endured the test of time. This view is consistent with Ansoff's (1965) opinion. He was also concerned with a focus on the industries and markets within which a firm operates and about which managers and leaders are familiar. We refer you again, however, to the sponse matrix (Figure 1.2) to obtain examples and a context of degrees of adaptation (followership) and/or invention (leadership). From these factors alone,

strategy practitioners can appreciate the extent to which corporations have built a culture of compliance and followership around real or imagined industry-specific boundaries and constraints.

For all the sense this culture of compliance has made in the past, our intent in articulating the notion of Third Wave Strategy has been to provide the strategy practitioner with choices. In other words, it has been to provide options in the place of a tradition of

> **strict adherence to prevailing industry forces and inherent industry rules which have resulted in a blind loyalty to strategies of adaptation and followership, leaving little room for the practice of prosponsive invention and industry leadership.**

If the philosophy of Third Wave Strategy is applied to its fullest extent and thereby requires practitioners to both adapt and invent, there is a need to understand what the implications of these forces are and how practitioners should re or prospond accordingly. In finding the balance between adaptation and invention, therefore, it is appropriate to once again refer to the two elements of external, Outside In, and internal, Inside Out forces that directly or indirectly have an impact on strategy and thereby firm performance.

Outside In, external influences

Meyer (2007) provides insight to our discussion from his research. When addressing the external influence of strategy from an industry perspective, he asked the question, "When a firm is capable of shaping its industry instead of following it, would that influence deliver a significant competitive advantage?" "Surely", Meyer (2007) suggested, "firms would benefit from 'setting the rules of the game' [*prospose*] as well as 'playing by the rules' set by others [*response*]".

The overarching objective of Third Wave Strategy is to be aware of the alternatives and then find the balance between abiding by industry rules or breaking them. It is our view that simplistic 'followership' of industry rules (compliance) is necessary in certain circumstances in which case adaptation is appropriate. It is also our view, however, that in circumstances where the rules can be broken without breaking the law and significant advantage can be gained by doing so then so be it. In situations where opportunities for competitive advantage are available, the potential exists to accelerate the firm's capacity to realise a *sustainable* competitive advantage (Porter, 1985), even though there may be inherent elevated but manageable levels of risk.

Of course, even a sustainable competitive advantage can decline over time. The antidote, of course, is to introduce a Third Wave Strategy option of developing a Program of Continual Strategy Renewal, as discussed in Chapter 4. This will at least provide an internal control mechanism that alerts practitioners to any changes should they occur. Through the adoption of this philosophy, it can be expected every business should give as much attention to the creation of its future as it does to its adaptation to the forces that are generated externally. So, far so good; however, the next question that must be asked is, "Do all firms have the capacity to reach beyond industry rules/forces sufficient to shape the future by inventing (and disrupting?) new opportunity?" The General Motors case study (Case example 2.2) provides insight.

**Case example 2.2   General Motors: external
influences on firm-specific strategy**

Founded on 16 September 1908, General Motors (GM) has faced many
challenges that have seen it exert a strong influence on its industry and
conversely, been subjected to harsh treatment from external forces. GM is
a good example of a company impacted by government-imposed actions
when in 2018 a number of initiatives were introduced to reduce the
balance of trade deficits between America and other foreign countries.
The government's primary weapon of choice in taking this action was
to impose tariffs on imports of steel from a range of global suppliers
considered to be taking advantage of North America's goodwill in the
international trade arena. Most striking to industry participants around
the world was the method of tariff imposition adopted by the government. Rather than go through lengthy anti-dumping/countervailing
investigations – and risk tariffs being overturned – UK TV broadcaster
BBC observed, "The US introduced tariffs amounting to hundreds of
billions of dollars under little used aspects of trade law". Citing national
security concerns, the BBC noted "Under President Trump the Government has taken sweeping actions to protect US producers by embarking
on a trade war, mostly with Europe and China, which he accuses of intel-
lectual property theft" (Levinson-King and Palumbo, 2018).

Following the introduction of tariffs on steel, its cost to North American businesses (such as GM) increased substantially. In GM's case, this
amounted to an estimated additional $1 billion (Opinion Lex, 2018) in
material costs a year. In its resolution to fight back, GM announced in
November 2018 that it would introduce initiatives that would lead to
$6 billion in cost savings as it sought to protect itself against an economic
downturn and the outcomes of the trade war. Key to the company's cost-
reduction program was the closing of seven production plants worldwide
and the laying off of thousands of workers in North America. This action
drew an instant reaction in the form of a rebuke from President Trump,
who had planned the opposite effect to this altogether. Fearing the worst,
reporters surmised, "Trump's response was to impose additional tariffs on
GM in a kind of reverse form of retaliation" (Opinion Lex, 2018).

GM, you will know, is today very much an industry follower, having stared
down a Chapter 11 bankruptcy filing in mid-2009 – a disappointing position considering it had been an industry leader for years. Although GM was
adversely disadvantaged by the imposition of a high-level external force in
the form of new tariffs in 2018, the company seized the opportunity to justify a plan that it believed would help rather than hinder its sustainability and

position of industry leadership. At that time, GM was very much preoccupied by the all-powerful forces of electrification, automation and digitisation. Just like many other car manufacturers, GM had become an involuntary follower of change and very much an adapter, not an inventor. The company has effectively been fighting to survive as it joined Ford (Case example 2.3) in the cessation of its previous mainstay core business: passenger sedans.

GM did not seem to be overly concerned, therefore, by the fact that the presidential decree had taken away a little bit more control of the industry that it had been so influential in making. Across the board, car manufacturers were scrambling to adapt while aggressive start-ups, such as Uber, Deliveroo, Tesla and even Google with its Waymo self-driving car were doing all the prosponsive invention.

New forms of external forces on competitive advantage

As technology takes us deeper into the world of automation, digitisation, social transformation and political transmogrification, another question to be addressed by the strategy practitioner is how to survive the forces that appear most regularly in the form of competitive advantage. Or is it? As witnessed in Case example 1.1, Amazon CEO Jeff Bezos stated that he is more concerned with emerging customer demand than with competitor activity. Rather than trying to beat competitors through engagement in extensive battles for market share, Amazon ignores them, seeking instead to learn from its customers. They, Bezos considers, are the ones who provide insight into future trends. They are also the ones who will pay Amazon money. None of their competitors will do that, he regrets (Kirby and Stewart, 2007). Of course, Amazon has competitors, and they do have an impact on Amazon's business – just ask the CEO of Walmart. Competition is everywhere, however, and increasingly emerging in strange and unexpected ways. With so much uncertainty in external markets, however, it's best to focus on customers first and competitors second. As Amazon profess, it is best to attune your technological resource base towards your customers rather than competitors, at all times and with a passion.

Third Wave Strategy and a position of 'fit'

Advances in technology, environmental sustainability, societal behaviours and convergence (the combining of different industry types) are now key factors in influencing changes in the very notion of competitiveness. In different ways, each are contributing to a firm's capacity to maintain and grow a competitive advantage from both an Inside Out and Outside In orientation. In many instances, a competitive advantage from early adopters of digital technology especially has led many mature businesses to their downfall. In other instances, disruptive technology has come to the rescue of many of those otherwise moribund organisations. That has occurred in areas where they have managed to establish new 'points of demarcation' between one industry and another. The problem for most mature corporations, though, is that it is not generally the industry incumbents that are quick to respond through adaptation or rapid instigation of prosponsive invention. Rather, it is newcomers such as Tesla, Amazon, Google and Apple that are leading the way with innovation and invention.

Consistent with this trend, clear distinctions within and between industries have increasingly become less certain. So much so, it appears that the sticking to the knitting philosophy proposed by Tom Peters and colleagues (Peters and Waterman, 1982) in the 1980s should now be heavily challenged. Rather than "sticking to your knitting", Amazon's Bezos suggested, strategy practitioners should embrace "the opposite: it's when you shouldn't have stuck to your knitting, but you did" (Lane, 2018).

The increasing incidence of convergence is one more, albeit recent, reason corporations find it so difficult to find, or worse retain, a position of 'fit' between its strategy and the external environment. The identification of such a fit was the mainstay of Ansoff's (1965) ideas and, accordingly, a golden rule of good strategy practice and scholarship (Grant, 2016). The adoption of opportunity created by industry convergence is also an example of the way in which businesses have been able to avoid being industry followers.

Inside Out, internal influences

There is a danger, however, that those in a position to adopt the benefits of industry convergence are unable to effectively 'reframe' their strategic thinking and thereby deliver a successful transformation project. When this happens, and it does quite often, they are bound to remain industry followers, not leaders.

As a result of the stringent legislation that has evolved since the global financial crisis, for example, financial institutions and banks, in particular, have been forced to rethink the way they do business altogether. Although they have overall complied with the demand for change (adaptation), they have still left themselves wide open to the threat of new competition. This is arising daily in the form of both 'fintech start-ups' and other mainstream technology companies that are doing all the invention. An example of the former is Bitcoin and the many other applications of cryptocurrency-based Blockchain technology that focuses on international money transfers. Examples of the latter are Apple Pay and more recently Facebook's proposed Libra cryptocurrency. In contrast, an example of a financial institution that has been inventive in this area is Dutch-based ING. It describes itself as a technology company more than a bank.

In optimising the resource set, therefore, and in overcoming an inability to reframe, we explore in Chapter 4 details of the concept of the SMI's Cycle of Organisational Transformation and Renewal. This concept depicts a sequence of events that helps organisations to avoid the pitfalls of random restructuring and instead define a pathway to a state of regeneration – the equivalent, if you like, of a state of high performance, at worst, and hyper-high performance at best.

Conducting a program of organisational transformation and renewal

The initiation of a program of organisational transformation and renewal is, more than anything, not easy to do. Ford provides a useful representation of an organisation that has recognised the need to transform as a result of disruptive change and the arrival of converging technology in its industry. As mentioned previously, the Ford story starts with the fairly dramatic announcement that it would cease production of its previous mainstay in the automotive industry: passenger sedans. The initiator of that decision was new CEO Jim Hackett, who had been appointed to the role in 2018. Ford declared that under its new manifesto, it saw itself transforming from a product-focused car company to that of an integrated mobility systems company. Details of the proposed transformation are presented in Case example 2.3.

Case example 2.3   Redefining Long Term Strategy, Ford Motor Company

In 1903, automotive entrepreneur Henry Ford and six prospective stockholders signed the paperwork that would incorporate the Ford Motor Company. Little did they know at that time just how successful Ford would become. Nor did they appreciate the enormity of the role it would play in the provision of passenger sedans to the mass market – and in the realisation of its purpose and mission.

All that would change, however, in 2014, when the 4IR brought with it the capacity for digitalisation of all things associated with the manufacture, sale and distribution and, indeed, use of passenger cars. By the time 2018 rolled around, Jim Hackett, the newly appointed CEO, announced, "Ford's point of view about the future of the business would be: 'smart vehicles in a smart world'" (Safian, 2018).

Building on the idea of transforming to a mobility company, Hackett was gifted the opportunity to fund Ford's transformation program by boosting overall profitability as he sought to focus soleley on the high volume and high value sales of its most popular and profitable products: F100 pickups, the Mustang sports car and a full range of the popular sports utility vehicles (SUVs). In Ford's 2018 annual report, Chairman William Clay Ford Jr. summed up the company's proposed transformation as follows:

> As we reinvent our business for the future, we remain committed to achieving strong results in the present. The future we are building at our new mobility campus is rooted in our past. Our mission then

was to "make people's lives better by making mobility accessible and affordable". That remains our mission today.

As we move through the 21st century we are reimagining what mobility will look like. That means not just smart cars, but also smart roads, smart parking, smart public transit systems, and ways for them all to talk to one another. To make this vision a reality we are working with and investing in all kinds of new businesses, from radar and mapping technologies to artificial intelligence platforms.

Of course, Ford isn't alone in this newly created industry space. Existing competitors in the automotive industry are also evaluating their options, while start-ups such as Tesla and Byton cannot be ignored. In a broader sense, technology companies Apple and Alphabet are also potential competitors, as are personal transport companies Lyft, Ola and Uber. No doubt there are many others waiting in the wings – that is the reality of the story behind the notion of Third Wave Strategy.

Not all companies are willing or able to benefit from such opportunity and freedom as that presented in the Ford case (Case example 2.3). To this extent, it is likely that some companies will find it harder than others to embark on the journey that Ford is attempting to do. That is why it is useful to understand the power of each of the elements of Long Term Strategy and the way in which 1) one element relates to another, 2) internal forces of alignment act and interact with each of the many aspects of strategy and 3) the cause and effect consequences of conflict arising from the tensions generated by the opposites of Inside Out vs. Outside In will impact strategic preferences.

An assessment of these and the numerous other ways in which internal and external forces impact strategy are readily identified through an analysis of relevant boundaries of a company-specific Strategic Architecture.

Operation and management of a Strategic Architecture

To explain the working of a Strategic Architecture, an illustration designed for its specific application to the restaurant industry appears in Figure 2.1. At a corporate level, the architecture is mostly concerned with issues of industry and beyond. At a business unit level, strategy is mostly concerned with markets, customers and business unit–specific or corporate-wide resources. The format of the Strategic Architecture is identical for both Long and Short Term Strategies. The term we apply to the Short Term Strategy version is that of a Strategy Blueprint (Chapter 3). You will observe in Figure 2.1 that McDonald's and Starbucks,

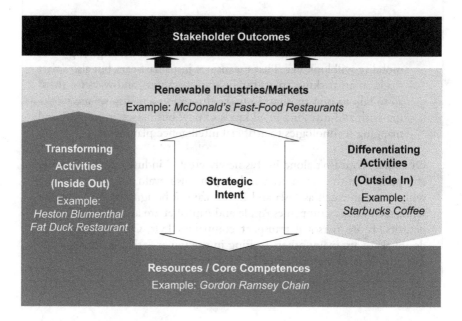

Figure 2.1 An example of a Strategic Architecture of relevance to the restaurant industry

as consumer-facing businesses and as divisions of global corporations, exhibit characteristics of an Outside In strategic position. McDonald's strategy focuses on market positioning, which is clearly that of families, teenagers and young adults. McDonald's service offering features a consistent and welcoming look and feel that includes a special appeal to children in its physical representation and design. It satisfies busy singles and parents in its offer of a fast, efficient service that is made possible via its large investment in on-premise cooking facilities. From a market perspective, its products are competitively priced. Its overall service can be described as the provision of comfort foods, entertainment and easy options for eat in or takeaway.

Starbucks is also a market-focused restaurant chain. In order to compete with the multitude of coffee shops that surround it, it has found a point of differentiation with its style, format and range of coffee options. Its target market is teenagers, mature singles and all adults. To stay in the game, it ensures that its customers enjoy good coffee, a good experience and access to facilities that provide a 'casual', homely feel in its 'almost a restaurant' environment. At the same time, they hold back on investing in on-premise cooking.

The Gordon Ramsey restaurant chain and Heston Blumenthal's Fat Duck on the other hand (in their context as combined corporates and business units) exhibit attributes of an Inside Out strategic positioning. The Gordon Ramsey restaurant chain is concerned with leveraging its specialist, highly skilled and highly motivated personnel and other resources into fine dining, mainstream restaurants. Restaurants in this group can be described as high-priced, high-quality providers of fine food and wine, which is served in refined, sophisticated environments. The more appealing the Ramsey resource base, the more impactful the result.

Heston Blumenthal's Fat Duck and associated restaurants on the other hand rely on high-level transforming activities as the basis for its considerable and sustainable competitive advantage. The Fat Duck, located just outside London, takes the resource-based option adopted by the Gordon Ramsey chain to the next level. Rather than fine dining alone, Blumenthal deploys a virtual science laboratory in his pursuit of a never-ending engagement in the conduct of transforming activities. His objective has always been to improve on the method, style, taste, texture and (in his case especially) magic of fine dining. Dining at the Fat Duck restaurant is a journey that lasts a day rather than an hour or two.

In the middle of the Strategic Architecture, the statement of Strategic Intent is not so much a characteristic of strategy but rather (also demonstrated in Figure 2.1) a description of the basis upon which strategy content is shaped and delivered. A Strategic Intent, therefore, refers to the fundamental and underlying purpose of Long Term Strategy but not the underlying purpose of the organisation.

The Strategic Architecture as a tool of Deliberate Disruption

Many businesses will inhabit more than one component of the Strategic Architecture. Organisations in this circumstance can be observed to be exercising a broad-based approach to the balance between an Inside Out and Outside In form of positioning when structuring strategy. It is in this area perhaps that digitalisation will have the greatest impact on an organisation's capacity to assume a sponsive position of Deliberate Disruption.

> *If there is one impact that digital technology can have on a firm's capacity to evolve a strategy of Deliberate Disruption, it is through a physical construct that we refer to as an Integrated Value System.*

Integrated Value System

As demonstrated in Figure 2.2, an Integrated Value System is evolved from the physical alignment of an Outside In, customer-focused Dynamic Market System and an Inside Out, resource-focused Core Competence Platform. It is our view that

> *an Integrated Value System has the capacity to support both an inimitable resource base and a compelling renewable and impregnable market position upon which an organisation can establish an unassailable point of differentiation.*

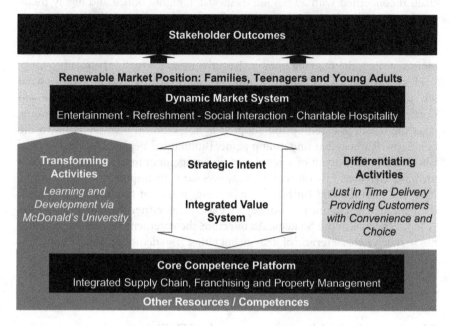

Figure 2.2 An Integrated Value System of relevance to McDonald's fast-food restaurants

Each are defined as follows:

Dynamic Market System

A network of related service offerings centred on the mainstay market position. As discussed previously and demonstrated in Figure 2.2, McDonald's does a lot more than just sell hamburgers. Its combined service offering provides its patrons with a mix of entertainment, refreshment, social interaction and charitable hospitality. McDonald's differentiates itself from other restaurants through its offer of convenience, dependability, consistency and cost. A Dynamic Market System can operate as an independent entity, or it can be integrated with a Core Competence Platform to make it a fully aligned and Integrated Value System.

Core Competence Platform

A Core Competence Platform is a mechanism that combines tangible and intangible resources (including core competences) into a single platform. Its existence can be as a solo but powerful resource base, or it can provide the foundation upon which a Dynamic Market System operates and hence an Integrated Value System is formed. The Core Competence Platform that is present in McDonald's is its integrated and extremely lean supply chain. It is an end-to-end supply chain that starts in the fields and paddocks and doesn't stop until it gets to the hot plate where the burgers are cooked. This competence is supported by additional competences in property acquisition and management and a capability in franchise management.

These assets are maintained and enhanced via a suite of transforming activities. They include the continual improvement of its lean operating capability and organisational learning and development programs. The latter are delivered via McDonald's Hamburger University. According to Walters (2015), "Hamburger University focuses on leadership development, business growth, and operations procedures, with a special emphasis on service, quality, and cleanliness to help prepare students for managerial positions in the restaurant industry".

Another example of an operational Integrated Value System is, again, Amazon. In its strategy and structure, it effectively leverages a Core Competence Platform consisting of a lean supply chain based on a technology platform that is reliant on a continuing alignment between suppliers and customers. The Amazon system is represented by a network of related service offerings centred on the Dynamic Market System that is in turn supported by the Amazon Prime technology customer management system. Everything Amazon does is wrapped in an overriding culture of passionate customer centricity. Maintenance of the 'promise' and trust upon which its customer relationship is grounded is dependent on an ever-evolving and improving Core Competence Platform.

It is not essential for an organisation to possess a Dynamic Market System, Core Competence Platform or a combined Integrated Value System to engage in a strategy of Deliberate Disruption.

It is our observation, however, that those organisations that do operate an Integrated Value System will have a higher propensity than most to evolve into a Hyper – HPO.

Nor is it essential for an Integrated Value System to be grounded in a technological platform. An example of a company that isn't is Eataly Delicatessens. A description of the make-up of Eataly's Integrated Value System and other examples of Integrated Value Systems are illustrated in Table 2.1.

To build an Integrated Value System, its features and construct become apparent through its positioning within the context of the SMI Model of Dynamic Strategic Equilibrium.

SMI Model of Dynamic Strategic Equilibrium

Representative of an extension of the application of the concept of a Strategic Architecture to practice a matrix can be evolved that provides the strategy practitioner with insight into alternative 'positioning' options. As demonstrated

Table 2.1 Companies exhibiting characteristics of an Integrated Value System

Company	Integrated Value System	
	Inside Out: Core Competence Platform	Outside In: Dynamic Market System
Eataly Delicatessens	Best products at lowest prices and food education	Diverse selection of quality food and drink
Burberry	Design and manufacture of high-end fashion items	Trench coat–centric fashion accessory system
Berkshire Hathaway	Financial expertise in merger and acquisition (M&A) and ongoing management	Fluid portfolio of efficient and effective companies
Cirque du Soleil	Integrated global supply chain with excellence in performance standards	Combination of dance, circus and opera in an atmosphere of a 'big tent'

in Figure 2.2, an Inside Out and/or Outside In perspective of strategy is combined to demonstrate ways in which either option can provide the corporation with alternative choices in order to arrive at a point of equilibrium. The model we have designed to reflect that third alternative is the SMI Model of Dynamic Strategic Equilibrium.

As it is a generic model, you can observe the various positions within which a firm is located within the zones that are found in the Strategic Architecture. The x-axis represents an extremity of transforming activities, resources and competences. These demonstrate the constraints of the limits to growth that are on offer, depending on the degree of the Inside Out strategic positioning chosen by the relevant strategy practitioner. Each are limited to a single dimension or can be expanded in accordance with the extent of each possible and chosen combination. The same is true for the y-axis, but in this case, the market positions show a limitation to the firm's capacity to grow. That capacity is enhanced through the addition of differentiating activities which provide an additional source of sustainable competitive advantage. Full equilibrium is achieved once a balance between each of the dimensions of the Strategic Architecture are reached.

As an illumination of the construct presented in Figure 2.3 – that is, the Strategic Architecture that was applied to the restaurant industry in Figure 2.1 – you will notice that McDonald's is closest to the point of a strategic equilibrium. This is the point where all of the choices that the four elements of the Strategic Architecture provide are deployed to strategy in practice. This observation demonstrates how and where an organisation can develop a more balanced approach to its strategic positioning. The examples included in Figure 2.3, Starbucks, Fat Duck and the Gordon Ramsey Group, are now in a position to appreciate areas where the incorporation of other characteristics of Long Term Strategic positioning could potentially enhance the growth prospects of their businesses.

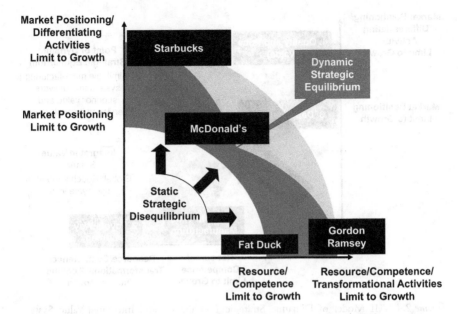

Figure 2.3 An example of the SMI Model of Dynamic Strategic Equilibrium of relevance to the restaurant industry

Extending beyond a sustainable, or even renewable, competitive advantage, Third Wave Strategy deploys the SMI Model of Dynamic Strategic Equilibrium to illustrate areas upon which an Integrated Value System can be formed.

Operation of an Integrated Value System at Toyota

An Integrated Value System provides a competitive advantage that is not only hard to copy and subsequently follow in the marketplace but also has the potential to significantly reduce competition because of its strength of customer appeal and effectiveness of its operations.

Japanese automotive company Toyota is a standout example of a company that has reached a strategic equilibrium through the establishment of an Integrated Value System. Even when operating in a reasonably commoditised industry, Toyota has succeeded in maintaining a sustainable competitive advantage by securing the following:

A Dynamic Market System

This is based on a systemic, broad–based market presence consisting of value (price and quality of its cars), durability, serviceability, availability and dependability.

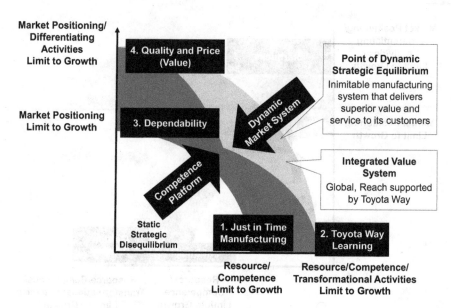

Figure 2.4 SMI Model of Dynamic Strategic Equilibrium and Integrated Value System applied to Toyota

A sound and robust Core Competence Platform

Toyota has long been recognised for its prowess in manufacturing, an accomplishment first realised via its philosophy of continuous improvement and just-in-time manufacturing methodology. That management practice is ingrained into the Toyota culture through rigid adherence to the in-house management doctrine of Kaizen – that is, the name given to the formal program of continuous improvement. Ultimately, the embedded and formal learning management practice that incorporates culture, learning and values is the Toyota Way. This is a practice that is constantly engendered, informed and disseminated by formal education programs. As presented on the Toyota Company website, the Toyota Way 2001 "clarifies the values and business methods that all employees should embrace in order to carry out the Guiding Principles at Toyota throughout the company's global activities" (Toyota, 2001).

As illustrated in Figure 2.4, Toyota is an example of an organisation that has reached the point of equilibrium in the SMI Model of Dynamic Strategic Equilibrium, as well as its realisation as a practitioner of an Integrated Value System.

3 Reinventing Strategic Planning

Thematic setting: *Shaping and reviewing Short Term Strategy*
Ansoff's contribution: *Empirical research into strategy has evolved into a bountiful library of first and second wave strategy tools and techniques. Most strategy practices, however, are still grounded in Ansoff's static strategic planning methodology*

Introduction: the notion of Strategy Evaluation

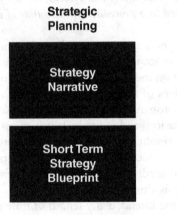

Our main objective in writing this book was to take an old, broken and outdated workhorse and remaster it into an instrument of the future. In evolving the design of a remastered program, our purpose was quite different to Ansoff's. His objective was to compile a workable framework that would help practitioners mould a broad range of disparate concepts into a structured but static and deliberate corporate-wide strategic plan. This would be managed, he thought, independently of day-to-day activities and would be reworked annually in accordance with a one- to five-year planning cycle.

In our remastering of strategy, the systemic, fully integrated Third Wave Strategy framework resolves many of the deficiencies in Ansoff's methodology. It also provides the means to fill the abundancy of gaps that can be found within Ansoff's truncated planning regime. By truncated we mean that Ansoff's methodology stops once (short term) strategy formulation is complete. That means, of course, that no consideration is given to any of the aspects that go with strategy implementation, evaluation and alignment.

Our use of the systemic approach to strategy is grounded in observations made by Senge (1990), who proposed in his book *The Fifth Discipline* that systems thinking "provides connectedness, structure and boundaries to our thinking" (which in this case is focused very much on strategic thinking). Boundary judgements, he suggested, "help people to formulate viewpoints about issues and dilemmas they experience". These viewpoints, he thought, would, "allow us to learn within the unknowable". Learning within the unknowable, Senge continued, "is a way to explore the whole as a means to connect the abundance of events that would otherwise appear to be distinct in space and time". This, of course, is a highly appropriate description of, and legitimate contributor to, the management of Third Wave Strategy in its entirety. As an activity, however, Third Wave Strategy requires a profundity of analysis and a capacity for deep, critical, informed (and legitimately intuitive) strategic thinking, followed by bold decision making.

> *As a component of an integrated system, the act of systemic strategic thinking can be likened to a procedure akin to that of evaluation.*

The tools used to support strategy-specific evaluation are, on the whole, drawn from the second wave strategy toolbox (Table 3.1). One of those tools is scenario analysis, which on the surface appears to be a tool that helps us to evaluate alternative perspectives of the future. In reality, its value lies in the associated dialogue that will automatically arise from the discussions required to make decisions based on various and individual evaluations of those scenarios. Evaluation and continual revaluation of strategy concepts are necessary because, as Senge (1990) has also observed, a serious flaw exists in an ideology that supposes it is possible to predict a future with any degree of certainty – as Ansoff was want to do. "It is doubtful", Senge observed, "whether the results that happen today are those intended any length of time ago. It is, therefore, inconceivable to think that practitioners can realistically plan over any great span of interrelationships or very far into the future". So, Senge continued,

> *The more we try to think global rather than local the more we experience the resistance of complexity.*

There is an imperative, therefore, to not only establish strong and robust methods of evaluating strategic options when formulating strategy. It is also important to establish a method to evaluate the outcomes that may or may not remain valid once the assumptions upon which they are based, reveal themselves to be reliable or not. Apple took a big leap of faith in the launch of Apple Watch, for example, which against their usual measures of success could

Table 3.1 Examples of tools and techniques contributing to strategy toolkit

Tool	Details
Level 1: Outside In, external indirect: universally focused environmental scanning	
Political, economic, social, technological and ecological (PESTE) analysis	An examination of the midterm external environment (10–15 years) from PESTE dimensions.
Five Forces analysis	Identifies those econometrically focused 'forces' that contribute to competitive intensity in an industry and thereby the attractiveness of an investment in that industry (Porter, 1985).
Scenario analysis	Provide conceptual insight into 'imagined' perspectives of the future that represent issues of complexity and uncertainty as they provide insight into a distinctly possible and plausible (but not necessarily probable) worlds (Wack, 1985).
Level 2: Outside In, external, direct environment: industry- and market-level analysis	
Game theory	Game theory relates to a set of concepts aimed at decision making in situations of competition and conflict, as well as cooperation and interdependence. Can be applied in situations where two or more participants are faced with choices of action by which each may gain or lose, depending on what others choose to do or not to do. Provides many insights into the behaviour of oligopolists (Nalebuff and Brandenburger, 1995).
Business model	Constructed in two parts, a business model "Incorporates all the activities associated with making something: designing it, purchasing raw materials, manufacturing, and so on" and second, "Identifies and describes all the activities a company does to sell their goods or services". These include finding and reaching customers, transacting a sale, distributing the product or delivering the service (Magretta, 2002).
Value chain	Describes the structure of activities that are undertaken to transform organisational resources into goods and services and as an outcome, profit. The value chain categorises the generic value-adding activities of an organisation. They are differentiated between direct activities (examples are design, production and delivery of goods and services) and indirect support activities (examples are accounting, human resources, sales and marketing) (Porter, 1985).
Industry value chain	Identifying opportunities to share resources, capabilities and management systems across multiple businesses (Porter, 1985).
Competitive intelligence	Interactive competitor and industry-/arena-/domain-specific data monitoring mechanism maintained as an embedded (intranet portal) program that monitors strategies and activities of competitors and potential competitors (Calof and Wright, 2008).
The three horizons model	Provides insight into a variety of alternative futures – a focus on building and maintaining the pipeline (Baghai et al., 1999).

(Continued)

Table 3.1 (Continued)

Tool	Details
Ansoff product/ market matrix	The Ansoff Product–Market Growth Matrix allows strategists to consider ways to grow the business via existing and/or new products and existing and/or new markets (Ansoff, 1957).
BCG and McKinsey market share matrices	The initial intent of the potential growth-share matrix was to evaluate business units. Subsequent versions allowed for product lines or any other cash-generating entities to be assessed (Hedley, 1977).
Blue Ocean Strategy	Blue Ocean Strategy is used to determine where high growth and profits can be generated through the creation of new demand in an uncontested market space, or a 'Blue Ocean', instead of competing head-to-head with other suppliers for known customers in an existing industry 'Red Ocean' (Kim and Mauborgne, 2004).
Multidimensional scaling	Illustrative maps of consumer perceptions of competing products along key differentiating variables (Grant, 2016).
Conjunct analysis	Uses estimates of consumer preferences for particular product attributes to forecast demand for new products that comprise different bundles of product attributes (Grant, 2016).
Hedonic price analysis	Estimates of the price that consumers will pay for particular product attributes (Grant, 2016).
Level 3: Inside Out, internal environment: resource and core competence analysis	
Activity-based cost analysis	Traditionally a cost-management tool that enables more concise allocation of costs to systems, processes, goods and services. Can be used to redefine resources but also assess the effectiveness of resource allocation and strategy profiles, especially in the context of the SMI Model of Dynamic Strategic Equilibrium (Kaplan and Anderson, 2004).
Core competence analysis	Capacity for learning in the organisation, especially how to coordinate diverse production skills and integrate multiple streams of technology (Prahalad and Hamel, 1990).
Third Wave Strategy: addressing complex strategic problems	
Strategic Architecture, Strategy Blueprint and SMI Model of Strategic Equilibrium	An overview of all content of relevance to a firm-specific, long term Strategic architecture and short term Strategy Blueprint. Along with the outcome of deep strategic thinking, these constructs also provide insight into gaps in strategy, causality/ alignment between Inside Out and Outside In and the basis for equilibrium.
Strategic business intelligence	Technologically, mostly digital sources data of significance to the strategic future of the business.

likely have been judged a flop. Yet Apple continues to invest in it. Historically, Apple has demonstrated that it is not afraid to walk away from unsuccessful products; however, as evidence is starting to suggest, 'wearable technology' is finally increasing in popularity. In hindsight, is it apparent that an early decision to drop this product may have been a mistake. With better insight today, Apple can see a far more positive future for Apple Watch. They are still highly reliant on the use of foresight to make that judgement, however, about which there is still no guarantee.

That is why the adoption of a systems-based approach to evaluation in a context which Flood (1999) suggested enables us to "seek to achieve a balance between instrumental action (methods deployed) and experiential action (lessons learned))" is deployed in this book. Accordingly, the notion of systemic evaluation is applied to define how strategy is formed (the methods deployed being the array of strategy tools available to us from second and third wave strategy practices) and how effective strategy is in implementation and post-implementation (lessons learned). It is useful to test methods deployed because when strategic decisions are made, they are usually based on decisions and assumptions about the future. These are tenuous and unreliable methods at best. Rarely are they tested for continued validity, reliability or relevance, as mandated in the Program of Continual Strategy Renewal (Chapter 4).

Similarly, it is fruitless to wait three to five years for the effectiveness of strategy to be tested (lessons learned), as they are likely to have been rendered redundant by that time anyway. It is impossible to know unless some form of evaluation is conducted to find out. The sentiment of Flood's terminology for these actions does suggest that the former is an act of Strategy Evaluation, Shaping and the latter an act of Strategy Evaluation, Reviewing. Each are defined as follows:

> **Strategy Evaluation, Shaping:** Evaluation through instrumental action (methods deployed). An evaluation of outcomes from tools and techniques (e.g. scenario analysis, market share analysis) deployed to contribute to an update of Long Term Strategy and/or inform a short term Strategy Narrative
>
> **Strategy Evaluation, Reviewing:** Evaluation through experiential action (lessons learned). Essentially an evaluation of the effectiveness of the

- outputs from strategy and its capacity to inform a program of organisational transformation and renewal;
- specific systems, processes and methods deployed to update and develop strategy that is both long and short term in perspective; and
- an organisational learning capability and its capacity to capture lessons learned from both Strategy Evaluation, Shaping and Reviewing activities.

In summary, we can conclude that the purpose of systemic Strategy Evaluation, as the key component of the second element of the framework, is grounded in four objectives:

- Inform Long Term Strategy, and shape the way it is implemented in the short term – through the acts of strategy formulation, implementation and alignment.

- Provide the means of reviewing the effectiveness of outputs from strategy and the systems, processes and methods deployed to derive, develop and update strategy.
- Contribute informed content of importance to strategy, ideally in conjunction with a formal organisational learning capability.
- Contribute to the program of organisational transformation, renewal and regeneration that is the outcome from realisation of the firm's Purpose, Mission, Vision and its associated strategic initiatives.

The method of Strategy Evaluation is represented as a micro-system in Figure 3.1. In its entirety, it can be considered a form of reinvention of the process of Strategic Planning.

Corporate Strategy (Remastered) in practice: Strategy Evaluation within the context of Third Wave Strategy

The Strategy Evaluation micro-system represents the first step towards a reinvention of Strategic Planning. In its operation, we accomplish the following:

- Incorporate second and third wave strategy analytical tools and techniques into a strategy toolbox. Depending on the specific needs of each organisation, any of these tools can be readily deployed when engaging in Strategy Evaluation, Shaping activities. In an environment of significant certainty for example, it could well be appropriate to apply first wave strategy techniques and nothing else. In these circumstances, a SWOT and associated gap analysis followed by a deliberate five-year strategic plan will be perfectly acceptable. Increasingly, however, such a Utopian environment is difficult to find and, more importantly, even more difficult to sustain.

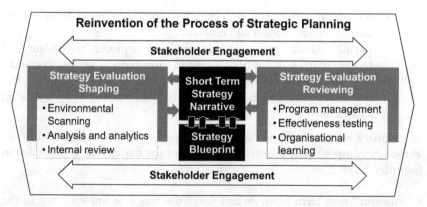

Figure 3.1 Strategy Evaluation micro-system as a representation of a reinvention of Strategic Planning

- Evolve Ansoff's Strategic Planning concepts into a construct previously referred to as a Strategy Narrative. The Strategy Narrative is informed by content derived from both activities of Strategy Evaluation, Shaping and Reviewing. The Strategy Narrative replaces a strategic plan but still provides details of the strategic reasoning that informs its content and expectations from proposed outcomes.
- Extrapolate (from the Strategy Narrative) the structure for Short Term Strategy, a Strategy Blueprint.
- Introduce the notion of Strategy Evaluation, Reviewing for the purpose of

  - establishing a strategy effectiveness review mechanism, and
  - formalising and providing content to a capability in organisational learning.

Program of Strategy Evaluation: Strategy Evaluation, Shaping and Reviewing

Strategy Evaluation, Shaping: getting the right content for strategy

Congruent with strategy formulation, systemic Strategy Evaluation, Shaping is conducted via the establishment of a formalised and rigorous approach to environmental scanning, feedback from internal strategic reviews and knowledge gleaned from relevant strategic analytical tools and other sources of knowledge and business intelligence. No longer will it be enough to focus SWOT, gap and market share analysis alone, especially on the activities of those few companies that when combined makeup the majority of the market representation. Instead, the Third Wave Strategy regime demands that a much broader range of knowledge obtained from a capability that can be referred to as strategic business intelligence. Key to this intelligence is the observation that competition is everywhere. Kellogg's, for example, doesn't just compete in the breakfast cereal market anymore. It competes for a share of the household's entire food, entertainment and health budget.

As illustrated in the Amazon case (Case example 1.1), a keen emphasis is placed on the customer and monitored through a strategic business intelligence capability. This intelligence is strongly supported by analysis and open strategy practices that are increasingly enhanced by the application of digital technologies. Examples include artificial intelligence, machine learning, predictive and 'big data' analytics. After all, our objective is to shape strategy out of many alternative points of view via captured knowledge, intuitive (or otherwise) assumptions and cold hard facts and figures. Of course, as with any analytical tool, a single focus (in this case the customer) can be dangerous. It should not be forgotten, for example, that customers are fickle and in fast-moving environments especially prone to a sudden change of mind, often for no immediately apparent reason. Similarly, customers rarely know what the alternatives are or what they really want. No one rang Apple to order an iPhone before it was invented. Nor did anyone ring Tesla to order an electric car before they started building one.

In the enabling of a Strategy Evaluation, Shaping capability, the establishment of a library of tools and techniques and instructions/teachings in how to use them will prove to be invaluable. This library (Table 3.1) includes access to second wave strategy tools, such as scenario analysis, market share analysis and digitised technology referred to previously. It also includes content that has evolved from internal research and experience. An example of this content could be the accumulated learning derived from the application of different 'sponses', which were discussed previously in Chapters 1 and 2. Their application could also be considered against the backdrop of associated strategic postures that were presented in the SMI Model of Dynamic Strategic Equilibrium (Figure 2.3). Another new model for review is the adaptation of the Strategic Architecture into a 'positioning' tool. As discussed and illustrated in Chapter 2 (Figure 2.2), it reflects the positioning aspects of strategy in the context of an Integrated Value System. Compare this approach to strategy practice with that of the MBA graduate charged with the organisation of a strategy away day discussed in Chapter 1, and you will understand just how bad her poisoned chalice really was.

Establishing a strategy toolkit

Systemic Strategy Evaluation, Shaping tools and techniques are normally associated with the activities of reframing, analytics, decision making, problem solving, learning, strategic thinking and planning. Their purpose is to generate information about relevant issues associated with the strategic decision-making activity itself. The objective of a Strategy Evaluation exercise is to enhance the value of strategy content and to ensure its relevance and validity. You will recall in Chapter 1 that examples of second wave strategy tools and techniques were identified. Many of these are included here as key components of Strategy Evaluation, Shaping. In Table 3.1 a strategy toolbox is presented. It provides a summary of well-known, mostly second wave, strategy analytical tools that have stood the test of time. Their continued relevance to today's business environment, of course, will be subject to change and continual improvement. To aid our understanding, we split the Outside In component into two levels of analysis. When combined, they become the following:

Level 1: Outside In, external indirect: Universally focused environmental scanning

Level 2: Outside In, external, direct environment: Industry- and market-level analysis

The Inside Out, internal level of analysis remains the same:

Level 3: Inside Out, internal environment: Resource and core competence analysis

A formal representation and establishment of the toolkit ensures that strategy practitioners are aware of all analytical options available to them as they engage in the Strategy Evaluation, Shaping activity. This terminology is applied here because the review process requires constant evaluation and revaluation if the content of strategy itself is to remain consistent and relevant. Of course, there are many ways to categorise and classify strategic tools and techniques; there are, however, no hard and fast rules about this proposition.

Strategy Evaluation, Reviewing: getting the right outcomes from strategy

As with open strategy practice (Chapter 1), Flood (1999) identified the role of systemic evaluation as a capability that "plays a central role in keeping all concerned people informed about key aspects of specific projects and helps them to learn their way into the future". Strategy Evaluation, Reviewing is deployed when it is determined that an analysis of a portfolio of strategically focused projects can benefit from frequent reassessments of their effectiveness.

The objective of Strategy Evaluation, Reviewing is to ascertain how well certain individuals or groups measure up to some specific objectives from the 'doing' of strategy – that is, strategy in practice. In which case it reflects on the effectiveness of strategic analysis, reviews and projects that are underway or have already been concluded. Its purpose is to capture and consolidate what has been learned through the process of Strategy Evaluation, Shaping and the implementation of strategy overall.

From a learning and risk management perspective, it is imperative that a determination of the effectiveness of content that is already a part of an ongoing 'live' strategy program has remained relevant, agile and viable. Typically, assessments of the effectiveness of 'strategies formed' have been flawed, as there is a natural inclination to wait and see what the outcomes are before an assessment of how good or bad decisions were, can be made. In most cases, this evaluation can take a year or more (five or six if it is a five-year plan!), and success or failure may have nothing to do with the strategy content itself. Yes, the fundamental strategy may be deemed to have been erroneous upon its evaluation, but it could be catastrophic for business leaders to wait years to find out.

From a management and control perspective, therefore, the imperative to make the transformation from static plans to a Program of Continual Strategy Renewal (Chapter 4), for example, is compelling. Not only does the nature of a short term strategic plan result in a loss of relevance very quickly, but its construct is anything but agile.

In fact,

> *it is our observation that the static nature of an annualised strategic plan physically constrains a capacity to engage in an Agile Strategy practice.*

Our reasoning is that when presented in the form of a static, deliberate strategic plan, strategy content is treated like a prescriptive 'wish list' of operational projects. Typically, these projects are deployed in the form of a five-year financial budget rather than a driver of systemic organisational change. Naturally, some of the key reasons errors in strategy occur are not always because of poor management or leadership. Rather, it is because of the very nature of the process. Fundamental to the conundrum of measures of efficiency of process in strategy is the fact that strategy is about the future, but the future is impossible to predict.

> *To make decisions about the future, practitioners are forced to make assumptions, and as we are well aware, the likelihood of an assumption being correct at any time in the future is far from certain.*

As suggested previously there is a need, therefore, to ensure that the evaluation of strategy effectiveness is focused as much on the assumptions and estimates that went into the decision making (maybe even more so) as it is an assessment of the value or benefit of the outcomes and results.

Regrettably, the dilemma of subjectivity doesn't end with a focus on outputs over assumptions. Another problem arises from the fact that the critical success factors used to assess strategy effectiveness may not be readily measured, compared and neither visible nor obvious at all. How do you *really* measure the value of a 12% increase in brand recognition, for example, an 85% employee satisfaction rating or a reduction of 25% in customer satisfaction? Just as importantly, how do you measure and manage the value and benefit of organisational learning?

Preparing a Strategy Narrative

There are no comprehensive rules that tell us what should go into a short term Strategy Narrative or how content should be developed. In general, guidance is provided through the adoption and operation of the Third Wave Strategy framework (Figure 1.5). Ultimately, it is consistent with content contributing to the support documentation that informs a strategic plan. Instead of being treated as a deliberate, static, one-off, annualised document, however, it becomes a dynamic, interactive, renewable, 'lived' experiential commentary. In place of a strategic plan, the Strategy Narrative provides input to the Strategy Blueprint, and this in turn provides the substance to the Program of Continual Strategy Renewal (Chapter 4).

Uncomfortable attributes of a Strategy Narrative

In breaking down our reliance on the strategic plan, practitioners should be aware that there are usually some very visible but generic guidelines that represent the preparation of Short Term Strategy in every organisation. Typically, they appear in the form of corporate-wide templates and standardised forms. These consist mostly of first and second wave–specific planning forms and documents. While there are many examples of step-by-step planning methods and worksheets, regrettably, these are rarely linked to other strategy-specific analytical tools and techniques, at least of the ilk discussed here. Similarly, these forms and documents are typically designed around a principle of Keep It Simple, Stupid. Regrettably, in strategy, there is no room for simplicity or stupidity. When committing an organisation to a multi-billion-dollar acquisition of another company or advanced technology, the decision has to be born out of some deep and critical strategic thinking and analysis.

In another context, it is apparent that there are a lot of generic business rules and regulations, about which practitioners should be aware. They will inevitably have a strong influence on our conscious and subconscious thinking. The influence of external forces is an example from our discussions presented in Chapter 2. Examples of generic business rules include generally accepted accounting principles, statutory demands and taxation decrees. For public companies, they include legislated behavioural expectations and mandatory reporting requirements. In Chapter 6, the influence of legislation that will challenge the very reasoning behind the role of corporations in society will be reviewed. This, it is suspected, will impose significantly greater challenges to business than is the case today. The risk of breaching the director's duties is also front and centre in strategic decision making at the board and executive levels. Similarly, there are often many company-specific, broad-based policies and procedures that strategy practitioners must consider as fundamental components of management and leadership responsibilities.

Regrettably, all combine to consume leadership attention towards a consciousness of things a business is not allowed to do over the much more strategic demands of things that a business can do. It is important, therefore, for those engaged in the act of developing a Strategy Narrative to be aware of oversimplification and issues of compliance and constraint; they aren't going to go away. Instead, it is expected that the distinctions between adaptation and invention, as key components of Third Wave Strategic thinking, will come into play. On the one hand, practitioners must be constantly prepared to deal with issues arising from matters and decisions taken beyond their control. On the other hand, they must be committed to a program of invention, inspiration, ambition, design, disruption and exploration – all items initiated within their control.

Establishing a Strategy Blueprint

This is the primary instrument that provides the pivot between the often distant, but essential, component of the micro-system that spans the topics of Strategy Evaluation, Shaping and Reviewing, the development of a Strategy Narrative and Strategy Implementation in its entirety. Both the Strategic Architecture and Strategy Blueprint are primarily used for the analysis of the construct of Long and Short Term Strategies, as well as illustration and communication. Their value lies in the fact that their preparation forces the strategy practitioner to filter out less useful content and include only the most important and significant information. Their construct also provides an extremely useful structure to strategy: What is in? and, where are the gaps?

If Lego, for example, doesn't recognise the need for a core competence in precision engineering, it would be very difficult for the company to convince stakeholders of its absolute prowess in the manufacture of high-precision plastic blocks.

The primary difference between the Strategic Architecture and Strategy Blueprint relates first and foremost to time. The Strategic Architecture contains Strategic Imperatives that will make the Long Term Strategy effective. As suggested previously, Strategic Imperatives are the "things that an organisation must have or do to deliver a firms desired outcomes and results – in the long term"; they will not change very much over time. They are, however, likely to be refined on an ongoing basis, but when they do change, they really change. Consider Sears, Ford and GM as examples of organisations seeking to implement a dramatic transformation to their Strategic Imperatives. At the same time, consider Amazon, which experiences continual organisational change but needs little reflection about its Strategic Imperatives.

The design of the Strategy Blueprint is based on the same Inside Out, Outside In format that applies to the Strategic Architecture. The Strategy Blueprint is similarly evolving continually, but as a live document, it does so at a much faster pace than the Strategic Architecture. In its representation of Short Term Strategy, it is made up of the specific projects that are the outcomes from the Strategy Narrative. These are the activities (projects) that are being actively implemented over the next three to five years. These projects are designed to deliver the promise enunciated in the firm's Long Term Strategy, but in the short term. An illustration of a Strategy Blueprint appears as Figure 3.2.

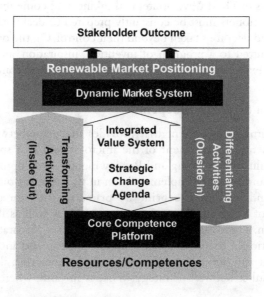

Figure 3.2 Illustration of a Strategy Blueprint

The following describes the difference between the two constructs:

- the Strategic Architecture describes those imperatives that a firm must *have* to realise its strategic ambitions, and
- a Strategy Blueprint reflects things the firm will *do* in the short term to deliver its Long Term Strategy. These could be reflected in firm-specific, unique market positions, differentiating and transforming activities and the possession of scarce or inimitable competences and resources.

Inserted in the heart of the Strategy Blueprint, is a brief portrayal of the purpose of the Short Term Strategy. This is referred to as a Strategic Change Agenda. This snappy, sharp description sums up the driving force behind a specific program of strategic change to depict its purpose. An example is "transform to an agile, digital corporation". At the point of Strategy Implementation, the notion of the Strategic Change Agenda is extended to become a part of the Program of Continual Strategy Renewal. This specific activity is referred to as a Strategic Change Program. In this format, it is representative of an action plan. Things that would likely be found in it are activity-based statements of intent and action-oriented wording either in or as an outcome of the Strategy Blueprint.

Assessing the human element of Strategy Evaluation

In one of the most significant departures from Ansoff's (1965) philosophies so far, it can be observed that Third Wave Strategy is as much about human engagement and deep critical thinking as it is a system-based framework. This is a capability that in turn is informed by the arrival of powerful data analytics software that is capable of supercharging our already operational strategic intelligence capabilities with augmented search and analysis.

It is proposed, therefore, that the idea of open strategy practice (discussed further in Chapter 6) be applied to the micro-system of strategy evaluation discussed in this chapter. It should also be sympathetic to an agile approach to implementation and alignment of strategy at a business unit level at least. Such a move carries significant implications amidst a fresh demand for the need for an embedded culture of organisational learning. In deference to the depth of strategic thinking required to support a strength of strategy practice it is referred to here as Systemic Cognitive Strategy Practice (SCSP). SCSP elevates the notion of strategy from deliberate intent to emergent conceptualisation of future outcomes and attempts to pre-empt them. In this capacity, it will be a key contributor to the practice of Green Shoot Strategy – an advanced form of Third Wave Strategy that is also discussed in more detail in Chapter 6.

Just as open strategy practice carries with it the promise of openness, transparency and accountability, SCSP is enacted by those who have the wherewithal to create, invigorate, invent and introduce strategic change. With access to advanced technology analytics and augmented intelligence capabilities, theirs is a capacity for deep critical thinking and analysis that is as much machine based as it is human based. To this extent, it is expected that a SCSP cohort will become a key component of a Community of Strategy Practice (COSP) and by association a division or adjunct faculty to a formal organisational learning capability. Accordingly, a COSP will be a part of a formal organisational learning function. It will have as its main constituents the CEO and other senior leaders. This would include as a mandatory requirement, the participation of the chief strategy officer (CSO) and her compatriots. It could also include learning and development specialists. Membership of a COSP is voluntary and would include a broad range of employees who will have a burning ambition to contribute to the thinking that is the driving force behind the shaping of their future.

The importance and inclusion of organisational learning in Third Wave Strategy

As early as 1990, Senge provided a strong impetus to us to accept the idea of organisational learning as a basis for the realisation of a sustainable competitive advantage. Systems thinking, he suggested, is a key component in the enablement of organisational learning. Systems thinking "promotes changes to fundamental, preconceived notions and assumptions as the basis upon which learning is carried out, problems are solved, and decisions made". A key attribute of organisational learning is as simple as dialogue – a concept defined by Senge (1990) as "the capacity of members of a team to suspend assumptions and to enter into a genuine capability to 'think together'".

Dialogue, Senge suggested, physically enables open strategy practice, and this in turn contributes to high performance. "Leaders who practice active dialogue will automatically communicate strategic preferences and choices in their discussions with individuals across the business". At the same time, all business dialogue is strengthened when strategy is clearly understood. Flood (1999) provided further strength to Senge's (1990) position. He suggested that as a primary contributing factor to organisational learning, systems thinking allows us to apply newly obtained strategic insight into complex problem solving. In doing so, he cited systems thinking as a way to define previously difficult to identify boundaries upon which strategic decisions can be based. This aspect of Flood's thinking was applied to the development of Third Wave Strategy. In doing so the idea of open strategy and the specialist SCSP was added to the notion of his systems-based organisational learning COSP.

Although this was done to help the strategy practitioner to deal with the "counterintuitive consequences" that unexpectedly occur when engaging in Strategy Evaluation activities more effectively, another benefit is apparent. That is its capacity to allow the practitioner to deal with the conundrum that surrounds all strategically focused work, the means to "learn within the unknowable". Flood's (1999) rationale for articulating this bold ambition for knowledge attainment is because the fundamentals of systems thinking have been found to generate a means to break down boundaries that would otherwise constrict our thoughts, specifically those associated with the dimensions of space and time. Once made aware of these boundaries, practitioners are better able to determine and envisage the 'big picture' and thereby structure their thinking beyond perceptions of boundary constraints that are typically held close to their chest.

The Third Wave Strategy framework, Core Competence Platform, Dynamic Market System, Integrated Value System and programs of transformation and renewal will all be beneficiaries of a systems approach to strategy practice, organisation learning and structuring. Each were integral components of Mars Chocolate's success when establishing a manufacture and supply business in China in the 1990s, as discussed in Case example 3.1.

Case example 3.1   Organisational learning as the key to success for Mars Chocolate in China

Introducing chocolate confectionary into China was never going to be easy, no matter how delectable and desirable the Western World thought, and still thinks, chocolate is. Prior to its introduction by the likes of Cadbury, Mars, Nestle and Hershey, few Chinese had ever heard of the product, never mind eaten it. Even if they had, it would have offered limited appeal. In a culture where the value of food is more important than spirituality and a philosophy of yin and yang prevails over everything, it was difficult for chocolate producers to know how to approach this highly attractive market. Fortunately, chocolate turned out to be a prescription for balancing yin and yang. It was, however, deemed to be a 'heaty' (hot) food, which meant it would be spiritually and physically difficult to sell in hot weather. Being first to market it, Mars recognised, would be an important factor in the realisation of a significant competitive advantage. Each chocolate brand/recipe carries varying flavours, and individuals usually get hooked on the one they first taste.

Both Cadbury and Mars sought to enter the Chinese market in the 1990s. By the time the 2000s had rolled around, however, the final stage of commercialisation in China in general was still evolving. Other than in big cities, the country's infrastructure had emerged from a state of disconnectedness. It was still, though, a world characterised by heavy government intervention, disconnected and treacherous physical supply chain characteristics and an absence of free and open market mechanisms. At the same time, there was a distinct lack of resources upon which any company could build a strong manufacturing capability – at least without a lot of help.

It was in this Inside Out, resource development arena where Mars scored an early and significant competitive advantage over Cadbury. While Cadbury laid down and followed a plan to build a manufacturing facility with the objective of selling "one Cadbury Dairy Milk Chocolate bar to each of the country's one billion people", Mars took a more measured approach (Allen, 2010).

Mars's strategy practitioners, according to author Allen (2010), applied a systems perspective in their development of a solution. In working through the challenges they faced, they recognised the lack of consumer experience with chocolate products. Accordingly, Mars focused on selling chocolate bars that were one-fifth the size of Cadbury's block and thereby one-fifth the price. In order to overcome a lack of appropriate human resources in the country, Mars also set about developing and implementing an in-house organisational learning and employee development program. It covered strategic topics in management and leadership, as well as operational topics in supply chain, sales and marketing.

With one eye on the future and the other on the here and now, Mars invested in the establishment of a long term education facility that would cater to the needs of the Chinese division for some time to come. So successful was this early initiative, the facility emerged as a formal entity referred to as "Mars Academy in China" in 2003 (Allen, 2010).

The result was a significant benefit for Mars. Just as individual employee organisational and manufacturing capabilities improved, the quality of products produced and sold were extremely well received. In contrast, Cadbury's less-organised and less-disciplined staff struggled to sell hit-and-miss quality, high-priced chocolate. When presented in oversized packaging, Cadbury sales volumes were low compared to the enormity of Mars's which ultimately realised a much higher market share – one that it still enjoys today.

This, though, isn't the only example of the value of organisational learning to Mars. In 2010, a new corporate university (CU) management team was announced. The objective given to this team was to elevate the profile of its service offering from one of disparate and disconnected networks to that of a unified and integrated organisation-wide CU. Consistent with its role, the newly emerged CU was expected to exert a strong influence on the change in strategic direction of the entire company. Launched as an action learning–oriented leadership development program, the newly transformed Mars University introduced a series of iconic programs that would appeal to all managers, from front line to senior leader.

The Mars case (Case example 3.1) gives credence to Shell strategy guru de Gues (1988), who observed that "the speed of learning may be a firm's only real source of sustainable competitive advantage". Many organisations have accordingly adopted the philosophy expressed by de Gues (1988) into their approach to strategy practice, as we do.

Organisational learning and Third Wave Strategy

When de Gues (1988) made his observation about organisational learning in the context that is interpreted here as being essential to a Third Wave Strategy philosophy, he was basing his views on his understanding of strategy and Strategy Implementation. When commenting on Royal Dutch Petroleum's merger with the Shell Transport and Trading Company in 1907, for example, he noted that this move was born out of a need for deep cost reduction during periods of economic hardship. The thinking behind the decision, however, was not just about cost reduction, he observed. It was also an example of clever strategic thinking that led to the initiative, providing a foundation for Shell's subsequent expansion into the United States in 1911. Insight into this strategic decision didn't happen by chance, de Gues suggested. Rather, it was enabled by the strength of the firm's leadership which, he observed, possessed a capacity to

> **absorb what is going on in the business environment and to act on that information with appropriate business moves.**

In other words, he suggested, it depended on their collective learning capability – a concept that he described as a capacity for "institutional learning". This, he described, is the process that enables high performance teams to evaluate and explore strategic options by openly "sharing mental models of their company, their markets, and their competitors". Ultimately, he suggested,

> **Shell thought of planning as learning and of corporate planning as organisational learning.**

Accordingly, Senge (1990) legitimised our replacement of a strategic plan with a Strategy Narrative and associated Strategy Evaluation activities. He also legitimised our integration of planning, strategy and organisational learning into the concept of Third Wave Strategy practice.

The logic of this conclusion is not readily evident in many corporations today. Regrettably, it is our observation that individual learning assumes a much higher priority over that of organisational learning. More recent thinking suggests that type of learning is just as important as speed of learning. As an outcome, practitioners can expect to witness the transformation of organisational learning capability from speed alone to one of speed and smart learning. It should be noted, however, that the emphasis could be broadened to include both an input and output perspective of knowledge management:

> **In addition to the development of a business school–styled _teaching_ facility, corporations should also benefit from an open, knowledge gathering, organisational-specific _learning_ capability.**

Most corporations possess a formal or informal organisational learning capability. Rarely do they capture an interpretation of strategic or operational knowledge that is the ilk of speed and smart teaching of lessons learned, either independently or combined. How many times, for example, have you attended an organisational workshop or similar event to conduct some form of problem-solving activity, scenario analysis or situation analysis. Inevitably, at the end of the day, the facilitators simply wipe the whiteboard clean or throw out the worksheets – and lessons learned as well?

Organisational learning within the construct of a corporate university

When organisations do fund a formal corporate learning facility, it is increasingly structured within a format of an internally operated "corporate university". Rademakers provides insight into the form and format of such entities in his book titled *Corporate Universities* (Rademakers, 2014). Here Rademakers identifies and classifies three different kinds of corporate universities as school, college and academy. Each name reflects the level of maturity of the various institutions and the extent to which the learning and development capability is individual vs. group based, static or dynamic in orientation, rapid and smart in focus and adaptive or inventive in nature. Examples of each different type of CU identified by Rademakers follows:

- **School (enabling strategy):** Operations-focused training in fundamentals of business, the company and industry. Described by Rademakers (2014) as facilitating 'learning as usual', it resembles a school-like environment where the fundamentals of various vocations are taught. These could include positions of bus driver, pilot, fireman and so on. The Mars Chocolate in China case study (Case example 3.1) is a case in point. Mars in China used its organisational learning capability to enable the everyday to take place.
- **College (implementing strategy):** A college teaches strategically focused skills in a format that Rademakers refers to as transformational learning. Similar to what Mars Corporate University became, it includes topics addressing advanced leadership, management and advanced strategy practices. Seeking to introduce a program of comprehensive transformation and renewal, Mars Corporate University was itself reinvented in order to lead such an initiative.
- **Academy (integrated with Strategy Evaluation, Shaping and Reviewing):** Conducted in the format of exceptional learning, an academy is described as being strategically focused, continually disruptive in its thinking and oriented towards Deliberate Disruption. The conduct of smart learning is the primary motive of an academy's operations. Its purpose is to provide support to invention as a primary purpose and adaptation as its secondary objective. The resolution of wicked, difficult problems is also addressed in academies, making it the domain of adaptive and generative systemic learning capabilities.

  Similarly, Mars (Foods) Corporate University exhibited an indulgence in academy style teaching. It is represented through the company's establishment of a specialist unit within the university that designs special courses to resolve problem-specific issues.

A summary of the value system and value drivers of each of the three types of universities identified by Rademakers (2014) is demonstrated in Table 3.2.

It is useful to transcribe our understanding of each different CU type into the sponsive change matrix, as illustrated in Figure 3.3.

Table 3.2 Characteristics of CU value systems and value drivers

CU value system			
	School	*College*	*Academy*
Focus	Linking individual and organisational learning needs	Linking organisational and strategic needs to change	Linking needs from outside to organisational strengths
Primary process	Building and running corporate curricula	Building and running organisation development programs	Breaking down borders between departments and organisations
Knowledge process	Deploying expertise	Gathering expertise	Unlocking expertise
CU team attitude	Managerial	Intermediary	Entrepreneurial
Focus	Understanding of current strategies to be supported	Understanding of strategic changes to be implemented	Understanding of internal and external drivers of strategy
Knowledge base	Employee/ management learning expertise	Organisational learning expertise	Strategic learning expertise

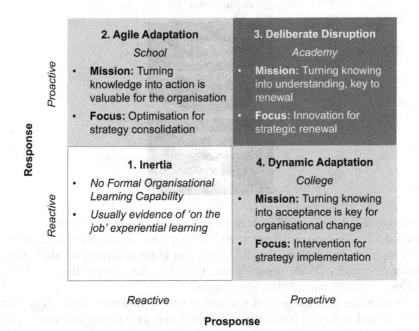

Figure 3.3 Categories of Corporate University types and impact on capacity to act as drivers of strategic change

4 Implementing Third Wave Strategy

Thematic setting: *Leading and implementing Short Term Strategy*

Ansoff's contribution: *Ansoff chose not to include methods of Strategy Implementation in his program of Strategic Planning, nor did he propose who should be responsible for its implementation*

Introduction: the challenge of implementing Short Term Strategy

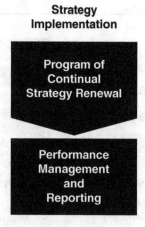

Traditionally, the primary role of Strategic Planning has been to provide a focus for the identification, articulation and development of the projects identified and approved for inclusion in (and subsequent implementation of) Short Term Strategy. Ansoff's (1965) objective was to define the content that should be included in the strategic plan, and that's all.

As such, the identification of a formal means of implementation, alignment, renewal and, indeed, appointment of a formal strategy function was never a part of his purview.

In a continuation of our remastering of strategy, therefore, those latter components of strategy were deliberately incorporated into a fully integrated system. In doing so, it brought a structured perspective to the table and an expectation that its operation would be embedded within an organisation's formal performance measurement, management, monitoring and reporting mechanism. As a secondary issue, it was also considered essential to introduce thoughtful and deep cognitive engagement as a principal requirement of the firm's strategic decision-making regime.

In the design of the strategy implementation program also, we address the contentious term of 'execution' and flag it as a concept of strategy that is erroneous. This term is contentious because it implies a circumstance of demise and most threateningly, an inferred pronouncement of death. This insinuation carries with it an inherent implication that once executed, the job is done, and no further work is required, but *nothing could be further from the truth*. In our definition of strategy, it is recommended that it be treated as a continuation of strategic thinking rather than a one-off event. As a description of a continual, transformational journey, therefore, it is stressed that strategy is implemented rather than executed. That's because the

implementation of Short Term Strategy is a part of a bigger picture, that of a driver of positive, continual change rather than a 'wish list' of special projects to be ticked off and buried.

This makes strategy an essential component of a never-ending journey to the future. A journey that is conducted in the form of a Program of Continual Strategic Transformation and Renewal. At its worse, the prevailing notion of implementation is contained within what could have been in Ansoff's mind – an expectation that it would be a task that is arbitrarily handed out to an unsuspecting business unit or departmental manager to complete.

Following the elimination of many middle managers' 'overseeing' role in organisational structures in recent times, permanent strategy roles have emerged and responsibility for implementation assigned to them. Here again, however, such roles have been highly transient and unclear in definition. As a result, consistency has been difficult to maintain. Just think of the task given to the MBA graduate in Chapter 1.

Our objective in this chapter is to assuage confusion about the notion of Strategy Implementation. Accordingly, presented in Figure 4.1 is a shamelessly process-oriented mechanism that we refer to as the Program of Continual Strategy Renewal.

There is, of course, much more to effective Strategy Implementation than a process or system, especially for those seeking to obtain a standard of Hyper – High Performance. As discussed in Chapter 2, de Waal (2010) observed not unsurprisingly that a strength in strategy is a common theme

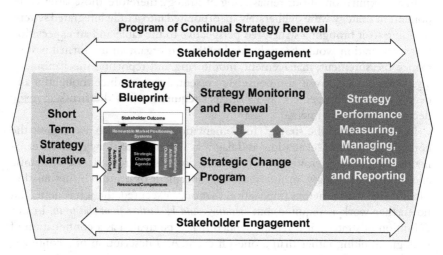

Figure 4.1 A process of Strategy Evaluation, Shaping and implementation: construct of a Program of Continual Strategy Renewal

and primary contributor to high performance. In addition to strategy, though, de Waal also identified two other factors that are of interest to us. They are as follows:

Transformational change: "HPOs have a long term orientation and focus on continuously improving and reinventing their core capabilities". This is an underlying philosophy of Third Wave Strategy realised through the maintenance of the philosophies of adaptation and invention. It is also embedded into practice through the presence of an organisational learning capability. It is also a component of the fundamental design of the Program of Continual Strategy Renewal.

Behaviours: "HPOs have a great ability to adapt to change and are able to react quickly to those changes". In the sponsive approach to strategy presented in this book, it is recommended the firm assesses, understands and considers its position within the basic sponse matrix and accordingly, seeks to move to another quadrant should it be dissatisfied with the one it is in. The means to do so is explored further in a later section of this chapter.

In the following discussion, each of these factors of transformation are applied to the identification of relevant aspects of individual behaviours. Where appropriate, they are enhanced to describe a Third Wave Strategy approach to implementation.

Corporate Strategy (Remastered) in practice: content and context of Strategy Implementation activities

As with all good models of change management, Short Term Strategy is best implemented in bite-size chunks. All these chunks are grounded in short term priorities that will in turn be sources (or causes) of organisational change, transformation and renewal, or put another way, organisational growth.

It is important, however, not to have too many projects that are visibly on offer at any one time. The change program should be bold and brave, but too much content will appear to be daunting and off-putting.

That is not to say that the strategy team doesn't have a bigger agenda. As a program of continual renewal, however, the roll-out can be elaborated in steps. That is another reason why a Program of Continual Strategy Renewal is far more useful as a management tool than an overblown and challenging annual strategic plan. As a program of continual renewal, the content expressed in statements of implementation can be tailored to the importance and relevance to the strategically focused circumstances of the day.

Once the content of a Short Term Strategy has been accepted, an accompanying articulation of purpose is critical to its realisation, as is "a vision that excites and challenges". From our personal experience, we have observed rather negatively, unfortunately, that

a program of change for 'change sake' has a low chance of success.

Unless a change initiative has a relatable purpose, a well-defined objective and full acceptance and ownership by all stakeholders, there is no real incentive for individuals to adopt it.

This observation contrasts with the nature of Long Term Strategy, which is a slow-moving change agent. It is true that Long Term Strategy is about renewal, growth, health, prosperity and positive outcomes. At the same time, however,

an articulation of Long Term Strategy can hardly be anything more than a source of validation, aspiration, inspiration, motivation and articulation of purpose and intent. Long Term Strategy relies on words that are always too vague and too future oriented to contribute to the realisation of short term change in themselves, the details of which may never have been imagined when the long term strategy content was first envisaged.

Consistent with the Sears case study (Case example 2.1), it is stressed that the purpose of Short Term Strategy is to deliver outcomes, not concepts. Accordingly, Short Term Strategy articulates

achievable, and sometimes 'stretched', strategic goals and objectives that are fully intended to be owned, accepted and initiated in the here and now.

A Program of Continual Strategy Renewal: the enabler of long term transformational change in the short term

The idea of the Program of Continual Strategy Renewal is to enable the ongoing measurement, management, monitoring and reporting of Strategy Implementation. In practice, the act of implementation will see strategy projects become very operational very quickly. It could also see assumptions, estimates and guesstimates lose their relevance very quickly. Any monitoring mechanism must, therefore, become a central focus for the management and control of the business. It must also reflect the (increasingly dynamic) strategic direction of the business on a consistent and continual basis.

Elements of the Program of Continual Strategy Renewal

In the following discussion, a detailed illustration of the Program of Continual Strategy Renewal, is presented as Figure 4.2.

The starting point for the roll-out of Short Term Strategy within the Program of Continual Strategy Renewal is evolved from the Strategy Narrative and Strategy Blueprint. Based on the projects, directives and instructions enunciated in these documents, the development of a Strategy Monitoring and Renewal and a Strategic Change Program can be established.

Strategy Monitoring and Renewal

This system is aligned with and provides feedback to the actors involved with the activity of Strategy Evaluation, Reviewing (Chapter 3). Its purpose is to

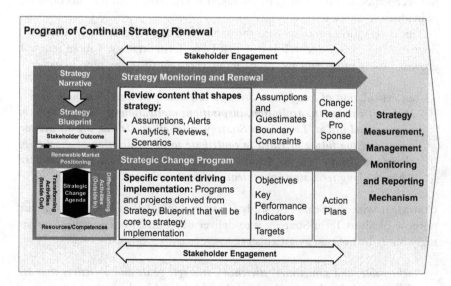

Figure 4.2 Detailed depiction of the construct of the Program of Continual Strategy Renewal

ensure that the content that is conceptual in nature, such as intuitive-based decisions, assumptions, estimates or forecasts, are regularly tested and continually validated and revalidated as appropriate. Increasingly, output from artificial intelligence and data analytics systems are included in this category of monitoring.

Ideally, content is also sourced from less regular performance monitoring sources than is the norm. In general, most content and data that provide the basis for management reporting are based on everyday enterprise resource planning, customer relationship management and internal, intranet-focused management information systems. It is expected, however, that further content should also be delivered from other less-regular sources. These may be internal or external to the organisation. It could, for example, be sourced from industry body data, search engine–sourced knowledge, internal analytics and other forms of web-based content. An illustrative control sheet depicting a sample from a Strategy Monitoring and Renewal program appears as Table 4.1.

Strategic Change Program

Sourced from, and linked directly to, the Strategy Blueprint, this program details all of the projects that are represented by the Strategic Change Agenda; this is the short, sharp statement of strategic change that represents the intent of the Short Term Strategy. For this, it is rewarded with its inclusion in the centre of the Strategy Blueprint. In this format, content contained within the Strategy Blueprint is quite literally a reflection of the specific Short Term Strategic programs and projects, as well as the associated goals and objectives against which key performance indicators, targets and action plans can be established.

An example of an illustrative strategic objective is "to become the provider of choice in healthcare". The details for each strategic objective are identified in the Strategy Blueprint and then related to targeted outcomes. Each are assigned performance measures and, from there, associated action plans, performance targets, names of those responsible and completion dates for outcomes identified. An illustrative control sheet depicting a sample from an agile Strategic Change Program appears as Table 4.2.

Strategy Evaluation performance measurement, management, monitoring and reporting mechanism

This is the final piece of the process illustrated in Figure 4.2. It is in effect a formalisation of the representation of the content flowing through and out of the Program of Continual Strategy Renewal. This mechanism can be fully automated and presented in a dashboard reporting format or contained in a more simplistic spreadsheet. When presented in a corporate environment, it is incorporated with an analytics based, integrated dashboard monitoring and reporting

Table 4.1 Illustrative program of Strategy Monitoring and Renewal

Content of Strategy Narrative	Strategic assumptions, guesstimates and estimates	Priority	Expected outcome	Current trends / outcome	Admin. officer
Adapt existing resource base to health services	All resource base is suitable for adaptation - Resource base is suitable for health services - Adaptation will result in cost savings No new technology is on the horizon	Very high	85% suitability 60% suitability 20% cost reduction Introduction of new technology when available	80% suitability 55% suitability 14% cost reduction New technology two years away	Josh Steinbeck

mechanism. As you will conclude, the focus of attention in this format is on monitoring, reviewing and renewing rather than administration, clarifying and report writing.

Adaptive and inventive strategic change: a Cycle of Organisational Transformation and Renewal

Strategy Implementation is decidedly a systems-based, project-driven exercise. Under no circumstances, however, can it possibly succeed unless it embraces and is conducted under the umbrella of an appropriate organisational culture and an expectation and acceptance of change. Culture provides the values, commitment and tone of organisational effectiveness. An entrenched, positive culture and acceptance of change creates satisfaction and commitment. It accordingly makes any change management program far easier to do and far more effective when implemented.

In the past, there has been some confusion as to the value of culture over strategy. This is exemplified by the throwaway comment that "culture eats strategy for breakfast". It is our view, however, that

a well-articulated and meaningful strategy is the driver of organisational culture. It fuels aspiration, engenders motivation, fires inspiration, clarifies direction and defines the parameters of the corporation's purpose, ambitions, goals and objectives. Culture, on the other hand, is grounded in values and provides the moral compass to drive and deliver strategic change.

Environmental context of organisational transformation and renewal

In addressing the specifics of Strategy Implementation, it is useful to revisit the insight provided from an understanding of the differences between responsive and prosponsive strategic change.

Table 4.2 Illustrative agile Strategic Change Program

Strategy Blueprint: Strategic objectives	Assumptions and assessment of ambiguity	Projects from Strategy Blueprint	Current trends/ outcomes	Expected outcome and checkpoints
1. Transforming activities: Adapt existing resource base to health services 70% of the health division is already operating in the health industry. Our task will be to develop a new business framework and organisational design.	Benefits of efficiency, effectiveness will result in improved quality, lower cost base and each of the items outlined in the Strategy Narrative and business case that led to the decision to embrace the transformation **Ambiguity: High**	Design and develop health industry value system for: • Aged care • Hospitalised patient care • General practitioners • Pharmacies	Significant trend towards introduction of Third Wave Strategy practice, agile organisation structuring and uptake of advanced technology, in particular digitised technological solutions	All benefits identified in Strategy Narrative: agility, cost reductions, quality, speed of service delivery, faster product development **Checkpoint:** to be established at each point of project sign off
2. Transforming activities: Improve efficiency and effectiveness of core business. We expect to close around 15% of manufacturing sites around the world and as result reduce overheads, including headcount.	New technology deemed appropriate will be available and working when required **Ambiguity: High** Investments will meet TgI return on investment criteria of 15% for each piece of technology **Ambiguity: Low**	1. Develop plan to introduce production optimisation program 2. Evaluate opportunities: supply chain optimisation 3. Rationalise product portfolio	2% Site closures and headcount reduction by the end of this year Supply chain cost increasing by 2%	15% Site closures by 2022 20% lower headcount by 2020 Supply chain cost reduced by 10% **Checkpoint:** to be established at each point of project sign off

Sponsive strategic change as a source of strategic choice

In the matrix illustrated in Figure 1.2, situational 'as is' sponsive states were presented to depict specific positions within which an organisation resides. In that case, it was different forms of supermarket retail chains. In this chapter, that knowledge is applied to provide a basis upon which the momentum for change can be increased and the value in 'doing' strategy enhanced. To do this, the idea of sponsive change is recast and recommissioned in the light of choices that can be taken to improve a firm's position in the sponse matrix – that is, to use it as a leaver for change, a much more powerful application than an information piece providing insight into current circumstances.

To illustrate, consider occupiers of the Inertia quadrant of Figure 1.2, they are Coles, Tesco and Kroger. Each are long term players in the supermarket industry. Each have barely survived on occasions; at other times, they have excelled. One can't help noticing, however, that a degree of prosponsiveness has allowed globally recognised industry incumbents Aldi and Lidl to outperform the incumbents – year on year. The same can be said for Costco, Walmart and Amazon. It is safe to conclude, therefore, that there is some merit in pursuing some form of prosponsive thinking and physically introducing a Strategic Change Program in order to take organisational performance to higher levels.

You are now invited, therefore, to assess the notion of sponsive change in the context of a firm's capacity to understand the actions it must take to realise the

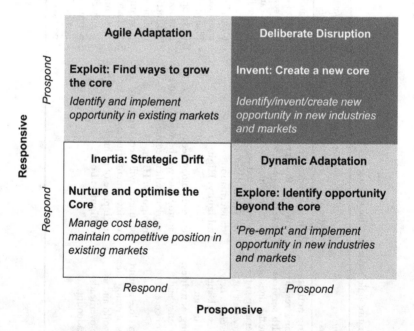

Figure 4.3 Four dimensions of strategic change driven by a firm's inherent disposition towards sponsive change

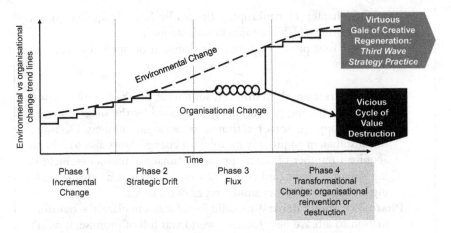

Figure 4.4 Consequences of Inertia, firms captured in a strategic drift

introduction and realisation of the delivery of a strategic change. As you will observe from Figure 4.3, this depiction of the sponse matrix explains strategic choices adopted by each organisation residing within each quadrant.

Each of these four elements of strategic change are discussed as follows.

Inertia: strategic drift – nurture and optimise the core

Business as usual would suggest that the best strategy when in a state of Inertia is to double down and to protect core business by managing the cost base and maintaining an existing competitive market position; then hope for the best. A regrettable outcome from this state of 'no change', however, is that a firm can be captured within a 'strategic drift' (Johnson et al., 2017). A strategic drift arises "when a company, responds far too slowly to changes in the external environment and continues with the strategy that once served it very well". Johnson et al. identify four phases of a strategic drift as shown in Figure 4.4.

Each of these changes are demonstrated in phases and in the form of a replay of the Sears department stores case study first presented in Case example 2.1 (see Case example 4.1).

Case example 4.1   Dilemma of a strategic drift at Sears

By the mid-2000s, troubled retail icon Sears was feeling the pinch from an onslaught of online incumbents, each vying for customer attention and sales. What followed next was a gradual decline that led to its final petition for Chapter 11 bankruptcy. Essentially, Sears had fallen into a strategic drift from which it couldn't extricate itself.

Each of the four phases of a strategic drift can be applied directly to Sears, as follows:

Phase 1 incremental change: As somewhat of a knee-jerk reaction to difficult trading environment occasioned by the massive rise of online shopping, Sears reactivated its catalogue business. Deeming this insufficient to provide meaningful change, Sears also sought to acquire a number of other apparently 'adjacent' businesses, including Kmart, a credit card company, a radio station, a mortgage lending company and other similar types of businesses.

Phase 2 strategic drift: With solid foundations in place, the transformation to a brave new (online) world was full of promise; it didn't deliver. Rather than adopting a plan of transformation supported by a newly minted supply chain capability, Sears instead lapsed into a state of stasis. This saw it run down its traditional shop-front retail outlets while investing in an online capability.

Phase 3 flux: Eddie Lampert, now CEO of Sears, explained his strategic plan in his September 2018 letter to shareholders, proclaiming Sears "was now a member-centric company and that through that lens, the Shop Your Way ecosystem will constantly define an integrated retail experience for our members". Still in its infancy, Lampert relied on income from its traditional, brick-and-mortar sales to support its transformation. Sears went into a steep decline, however, as vital investment funds were diverted to the new business while its existing businesses were left to decay (Peterson, 2017).

Phase 4 transformational change: organisational reinvention or destruction: Despite drastic efforts, Sears was unsuccessful in turning its business around. The outcome? This once iconic retail brand entered Chapter 11 bankruptcy protection in October 2019.

To avoid getting caught in a strategic drift, it is necessary to orchestrate a change in direction and approach to strategic thinking. Inspiration is available from those exhibiting the characteristics of Agile Adaptation, the next level of performance.

Agile Adaptation: explore – find ways to grow the core

This is an approach that is taken as an outcome from an expected change in the environment or is triggered by a recognition of a need for change, primarily in existing markets or from within. Accordingly, the primary change program is one that is focused on the identification of opportunities to improve internal operations and/or opportunities for growth in markets where the firm has a track record. Examples of an adaptive change in this situation could be a firm's response to the aging design of a specific model of car or white good such as a kitchen appliance. Another is the response to an acquisition of a competitor by another competitor.

It's always OK to be a member of this low-risk club, as long as that is not all you do. Many commodities-based businesses convince themselves that this is all they can do. They are mistaken, Amazon deals in commodities – it's all about prosponsive thinking and the enactment of Third Wave Strategy practice and, ultimately, an eye on the development of both a Core Competence Platform and Dynamic Market System. That is, the expected outcome from the state of Dynamic Adaptation, realised at the next level of organisational high performance.

Dynamic Adaptation: exploit – identify opportunity beyond the core

In this approach to strategic change, a degree of reframing is required to transform the focus of strategic thinking away from adaptation and more towards invention. Ultimately, prosponsive change becomes a more natural way of thinking at this level. Its consistent use prompts the high performing leadership team to 'pre-empt' and identify and then implement new opportunities. Their thinking is also fully aligned to advances in technology, social change and enhanced skills. All are deployed to explore and create new industries and new markets. This is a change strategy that is acceptable but still relatively conservative; it builds on a strength in adaptation but excels when a prosponsive invention is included in the mix. Those high-performance leaders already operating at this level and those inclined to progress to this level would be interested to learn about the notion of strategic agility. It is a form of team behaviour that allows high-performance teams, especially, to maintain or ramp up performance.

Based on research conducted into high-performance technology companies, authors Doz and Kosonen (2008) described Agile Strategy as "thoughtful, purposive interplay between three vectors of strategic modes of behaviour". The three vectors are sequentially those of strategic sensitivity, leadership unity and resource fluidity.

- Strategic sensitivity is an attribute of a leadership team's capacity to exercise a "sharpness of perception, intensity of awareness and attention paid to strategic developments".
- Leadership unity refers to the ability of a leadership team "to make bold, fast decisions, without being bogged down in 'win-lose' politics".
- Resource fluidity refers to a leadership's internal capability to seamlessly "reconfigure capabilities and to rapidly redeploy resources".

Jeff Bezos wasn't satisfied to simply explore or exploit opportunities in known or even unknown industry and market boundaries. Carrying a burning ambition to take Amazon to a level of Hyper – High Performance or more, he was keen to invent and create opportunity through the means of Deliberate Disruption and an exploration of multidextrous strategic change.

Deliberate Disruption: regenerate – continual transformation of the core

Third Wave Strategy practice is all about the identification and implementation of multidextrous opportunity seeking created out of an albeit higher risk adoption of deliberate, disruptive strategic change. This form of strategic change is characterised by a systems approach to strategy practice and organisation design, as witnessed through the construction and enablement of an Integrated Value System and the application of the concept of Green Shoot Disruption. Discussed further in Chapter 6, the characteristics of Green Shoot Strategy represent an outcome from an accelerated Deliberate Disruption of a system, initiated by an intent to create new opportunity in new industries and new markets.

A Green Shoot, accelerated, Deliberate Disruption is successful when it prosponsively creates a disruption that results in the creation of new business systems and potentially new industries altogether. As an example, Tesla first sought to disrupt the entire automotive industry. Tesla founder Elon Musk's objective was to introduce viable and highly attractive cars that deployed electricity as a source of clean, renewable energy as an alternative to dirty, fossil-fuelled energy. Unlike other automotive companies, Tesla did not adapt what it was already producing to the new opportunity – it leveraged its evolving competency in battery technology to develop a new battery capability altogether. As it invested in the development of a new battery-powered vehicle, it also created through its value-based, energy-efficient system a Green Shoot Strategy disruption that effectively led to a discontinuity in the energy industry. Not only was Tesla's battery energy storage system of relevance to the automotive industry. It was also found that it could be applied to installations in domestic and commercial buildings. In this system, energy is sourced from the grid, and off grid and stored in its battery systems. It is then drawn down on an as needed basis rather than one determined by the electricity distributor. Any excess energy is redirected and sold back into the national grid.

What quadrant of the sponse matrix is right for you? Here are the options in real life:

Inertia: No one wants to plan for stagnation or decline.

Agile Adaptation: No one plans to be ordinary.

Dynamic Adaptation: No one wants to overpromise; however, in practice, the chairman and CEO will agree to stretch goals and targets typical of Dynamic Adaptation. The chairman, however, won't stop the CEO from exploring the means to adopt a strategy of **Deliberate Disruption**.

This ambition is likely to fester within the leadership team whether the reality of achieving this higher order of goals and objectives is real or not. There is a risk, however, that at some point, it will all go pear shaped. The CEO is then made accountable, and the board is given a hard time. What approach do you choose?

> *The need for the adoption of continual adaptive and inventive change is paramount for those wishing to become Hyper – HPOs.*

To realise such an outcome, however, the obvious question is,

> *How can an organisation make the change from a current state of either Inertia, Agile or Dynamic Adapter – to that of a prosponsive, deliberately disruptive inventor that is the basis of a Hyper – HPO?*

Any solution is realised by degrees and is undertaken via an embarkation on a journey of organisational transformation and renewal. Thankfully, a program for such a journey has already been developed. It is referred to here; as the SMI Cycle of Organisational Transformation and Renewal.

SMI's Cycle of Organisational Transformation and Renewal

Our awareness of this cycle arose from specialist research that was conducted into the topic of strategic revitalisation by Hunter, (2001). In this research, Hunter was seeking to identify root causes and elements of success or failure in formal programs of large-scale organisational change. From this research, two key observations were made. The first is that organisational change generally does not occur in single-step stages of unfreeze–change–refreeze, a process observed by Lewin (1947) and practiced by many. Rather, it was observed that transformational change

> *is most effective when undertaken in four distinct phases of reframing, restructuring, revitalising and regeneration.*

It was also observed from Hunter's research that there is a distinct strategic lesson attached to the four-stage Cycle of Organisational Transformation and Renewal. It is

> *those organisations that emerged from a restructuring exercise (reduce costs, reorganise, downsize) that had no clear purpose for a (growth-oriented) future were less likely to succeed than those that did.*

On the other hand, it was also observed that

> *those organisations that had a clear articulation of what they wanted to transform to were far better placed than those that didn't in the realisation a state of regeneration.*

An illustration of the SMI Cycle of Organisational Transformation and Renewal is illustrated in Figure 4.5. Each element is discussed as follows:

Reframing: The act of reframing is an essential starting point for transformational change. Nothing will happen unless there is acceptance of the existence of a problem, a clear and unanimous understanding of what the problem is and a willingness to resolve it. There is no greater strategic problem, of course, than one where it is necessary for the corporate leaders to recognise and admit they are close to or at risk of entering a strategic drift.

The primary objective of the act of reframing is to reconceptualise the reality of the situation at hand and to rethink, reimagine and generally look at the world and the organisation's role in it from a different perspective. The primary purpose of this exercise is to take the time to define exactly what the future should be for the corporation. Once a decision to implement a program of transformation and renewal has been taken, the change program commences when the firm embarks on the second stage of the cycle, that of *restructuring*.

Restructuring: As stated previously, without a clear understanding of what the organisation wanted to achieve or become, organisations are unlikely to avoid or survive the trap of a strategic drift (Figure 4.4). Businesses caught in a strategic drift are generally forced to become commodity suppliers and as such are locked into a downward spiral of cost and price reduction as a sole means to compete.

We refer to such a position as that of a vicious cycle of value destruction

Revitalisation: For those that do succeed in restructuring, of course, an ensuing period of *revitalisation* must ensue as those employees who have continued with the corporation, as well as those who have joined post-restructuring,

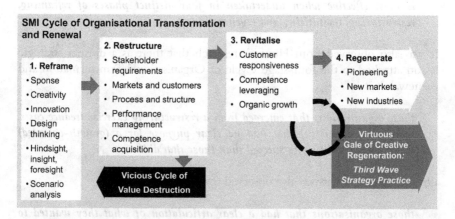

Figure 4.5 Stages and consequences of change in accordance with the SMI's Cycle of Organisational Transformation and Renewal

will be grateful for a boost to morale and a revitalisation of the culture of the business. The primary objective in this phase of the cycle is to capitalise on opportunities and to minimise any risk of reversal. The measure of success for those that have successfully transformed is their entry into a world of *regeneration*.

Regeneration: When in this state, organisations will typically be committed to a program of continual adaptation and invention. This means that the organisation is unlikely to have to engage in any form of major restructuring again. Their longevity will be dependent, however, on the management of the concept of deliberate change, a concept often referred to as Schumpeter's (1934) 'gale of creative destruction'. Schumpeter was an economist who, in the 1930s, proposed that a clear aspect of entrepreneurship is its ruthless commitment to commercial endeavour, with opportunity created by any means, including the act of Deliberate Disruption. A state of regeneration is a key benefit from the implementation of a Program of Continual Strategy Renewal. As demonstrated in Figure 4.5,

> *we refer to the phenomenon of regeneration as that of a virtuous gale of creative regeneration.*

It was also observed that

> *a Hyper – HPO exists within a continual state of regeneration.*

Developing a definitive Pathway to Regeneration

It is appropriate at this point to remind you of the true meaning and purpose of strategy and the necessity to overcome a perception that it is only concerned with the identification of the means to obtain a competitive advantage, finding positions of fit and the development of a strategic plan. These, along with other 'reasons' to do strategy are misguided and should only be considered to be subsets of strategy. Instead, we propose that the real emphasis of strategy is on the identification, implementation and realisation of strategically focused change. The primary task of strategic leadership, therefore, is to continually find the means to

> *realise organisational purpose through the continual implementation of long term strategy; via short term initiatives that are key drivers of change.*

An extension of our understanding of strategy first discussed in Chapter 2, therefore, would suggest that the purpose of strategy is to

> *describe how a firm will realise its organisational purpose through its continual adaptation to foreseen and unforeseen change and the implementation of opportunity driven by innovative inventions introduced as drivers of deliberate and often disruptive change.*

How, though, can these concepts be made to work in practice? A recommended answer is to combine the depiction of the nature of strategic change demonstrated in the sponse matrix (Figure 4.3) with the stages of change identified in the SMI Cycle of Organisational Transformation and Renewal (Figure 4.5). A predetermined pathway to regeneration soon emerges. Shown as Figure 4.6, a reinterpretation of the sponse matrix first presented in Figure 4.3 is used to illustrate a combined representation of the conduct of sponsive strategic change undertaken within the conditions of the SMI Cycle of Organisational Transformation and Renewal.

This newly defined matrix provides us with the means to define a journey for an organisation to transform towards the status of a *deliberately disruptive, regenerative Hyper –HPO*, thereby rescuing those who are

- wallowing in a state of a strategic drift,
- seeking to survive by not being left behind as the environmental change continues apace, or
- wishing to thrive by stepping out in front and creating their own future.

As a system, it doesn't matter where the practitioner starts in their implementation of change. The end game, however, for most will be to reach the stage of regeneration. The final depiction of a journey and state of regeneration that is referred to as the SMI Pathway to Regeneration is illustrated in Figure 4.7.

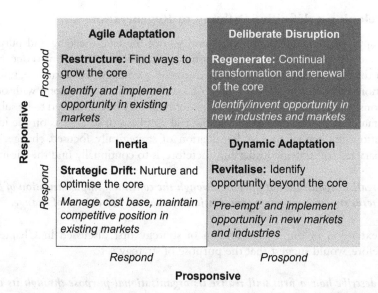

Figure 4.6 Combined dimensions of strategic change driven by a firm's inherent disposition towards sponse and elements of the SMI Cycle of Organisational Transformation and Renewal

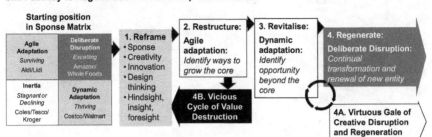

Figure 4.7 From static to dynamic: SMI Cycle of Organisational Transformation and Renewal as launchpad for Pathway to Regeneration

Implementation of the Strategic Change Program demonstrated and discussed previously in this chapter will always be a priority. Such a program, however, is not necessarily contextualised within the meaning and purpose of strategy that has been defined previously in this book. Practitioners are now afforded a contextualisation that exists within a system. It is based on our view that strategy is contributing to, and a driver of, the growth, transformation and renewal of the business, not the strategy itself. Of course, those wishing to simply continue what they are doing will still benefit from a newfound and comprehensive understanding of strategy. If they understand enough about Third Wave Strategy concepts, however, there is no doubt that the idea of Third Wave Strategy practice will be appealing. Either way, they at least now have a choice as to their approach to a positive way forward.

5   Strategic Alignment

Thematic setting: *Getting results from strategy*
Ansoff's contribution: *As a stand-alone, end-to-end process, Ansoff's strategic planning methodology was devoid of any conscious form of alignment, other than the often referred to position of strategic 'fit'*

Introduction: the mystique of Strategic Alignment

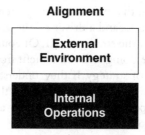

Our discussion up to this point has focused predominantly on the customer-oriented aspects of business-level strategy, much more so than the stakeholder-oriented topic of corporate-level strategy. Grant (2016) offers a distinction between the two:

Business unit strategy is concerned with <u>how</u> a firm competes within a particular market.

Corporate strategy is concerned with <u>where</u> a firm competes – that is, in what industries and in what markets?

In drawing your attention to the differences, the classic dilemma of strategy is immediately brought to attention: "How can alignment between each of these two dimensions of strategy practice be adequately maintained?" As the primary topic of this chapter, an explanation and understanding of alignment, or a lack thereof, is explored in detail. In doing so, it must be admitted that there is no real theory upon which a generally accepted definition of strategic Alignment can be found. One source of insight that is available, is proposed by Trevor and Varcoe (2016) who observed:

> *Strategic alignment is the way in which a corporation is organised and structured to support the fulfilment of its organisational purpose.*

In Chapter 2, it was noted that Mayer (2018), defined organisational purpose as "the reasons a corporation is created and exists, what it seeks to do and what it seeks to become". This definition is readily applied here and, in that context, is consistent with Trevor and Varcoe's observation that organisational purpose is a long term proposition and in this context is 'enduring'. It has been explained in previous chapters also that Purpose, Mission, Vision are enduring. We agree therefore with the sentiment expressed by Trevor and Varcoe that it is the role of strategy to describe how "a company's people, culture, structure and processes will be flexed and changed to deliver the objectives of an enduring organisational purpose". We now add, however, an observation that these responsibilities are actually the role of Short Term, not Long Term Strategy, as Trevor and Varcoe surmise. This is, of course, a distinction that you will agree would have once seemed trivial but is now quite the opposite.

To understand the Third Wave Strategy view of alignment, some relief can be found from a lack of definition:

> *As the Third Wave Strategy framework operates as a system, everything is connected to everything else. There is, therefore, reduced potential for a lack of alignment as a result.*

When considered in the context of the Third Wave Strategy framework especially, it can be noted that as feeders to the Program of Continual Strategy Renewal, both the Strategy Narrative and Strategy Blueprint are strongly aligned. Accordingly, it can be held true that Alignment completes the full loop between *purpose, strategy, structure* and *operations*. Just as we have followed in the footsteps of Ansoff to get to this point, however, so too do we refer to Chandler's (1962) observation expressed in his similarly aged book *Strategy and Structure* that suggested, "just as structure follows strategy, so too do product market characteristics create operating needs and these in turn determine the structure of authority, responsibility, workflows, and information flows within the firm". It us useful to adapt and extend a more familiar version of the foregoing to our ensuing discussion on this topic:

> *Strategy follows purpose, structure follows strategy, systems and processes follow structure.*

Structure and systems are encapsulated within the operations of the business. They are also defined in the strategy implementation element of the Third Wave Strategy framework. It is in this context, therefore, that the strategy framework alignment to the four elements of *purpose, strategy, structure* and *operations*. An illustration of the strength of this alignment against the backdrop of the framework presented in Figure 1.5 is shown here as Figure 5.1.

This is, of course, a view of Alignment at a Level 3, Inside Out internal perspective that was referred to in Chapter 3. As explored in the following discussions, issues of alignment at Level 1 and 2, Outside In external perspectives of Alignment must also be included in any analysis.

Corporate Strategy (Remastered) in practice: identifying the touch points of Strategic Alignment

Even though the strategy framework reduces the potential for the risk of misalignment, the imprecise nature of strategy will inevitably result in deviations and misalignments to occur. Accordingly, it can be expected that an outcrop of unintended consequences will inevitably occur from time to time, probably more frequently than not. Alignment within a consciously designed Integrated Value System, for example, will be easier to control than if it were a suite of processes or hierarchical constructs that are typically associated with first and second wave strategy practice. No matter which wave of strategy practice practitioners are working within, the general rule will prevail that says that to a lesser or greater degree,

> *the issue of poor alignment will prevail at the level of a network of major strategy systems or independently as part of a strategy sub-system.*

Misalignment may not appear at any one juncture, nor at any one time. Nor will it necessarily be all encompassing. It may occur at any level between the organisation and the external environment or wholly within the internal environment. A lack of alignment will, therefore, be felt in many different contexts and in many different situations. In broad terms, it can be observed that rather than being limited purely to the link between "the way in which a corporation is organised and structured to support the fulfilment of its organisational purpose" as Trevor and Varcoe (2016) propose:

> *the boundaries of Strategic Alignment are in fact fluid, dynamic, unpredictable and boundaryless. They can be found in many different forms and formats and in areas of questionable circumstances within any organisation.*

Identifying touch points of Strategic Alignment

To address the issue of uncertainty that surrounds the notion of positive or negative alignment, the notion of 'touch points' is applied to identify areas of potential vulnerability. Illustrative examples of some random or 'hard to find' touch points in broad terms include the following:

- **Purpose and structure:** An example of a touch point that is quite conceptual in nature is Ford's strategically focused transformation and renewal

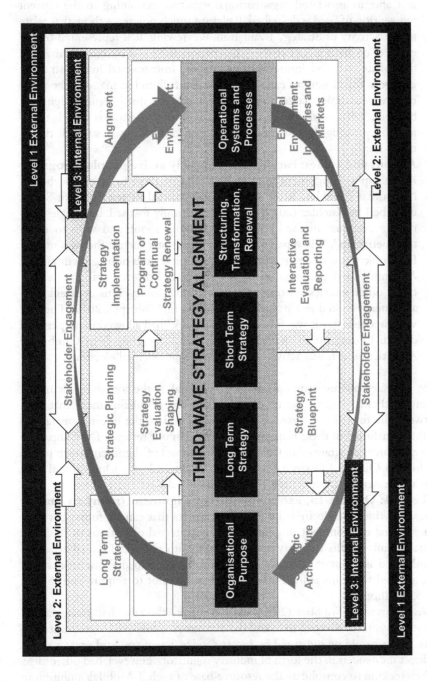

Figure 5.1 Alignment between purpose, strategy, structure and operations in the context of the Third Wave Strategy framework

program discussed in Case example 5.1. In this case, a future business format and an associated organisational structure pertaining to the current reinvention of Ford is described. Relevant touch points are those that relate to the activity of Strategy Evaluation, Reviewing. It is represented by the connect or disconnect between the corporation's past business format and that of its intended future business format. Instrumental in this strategic change is the closure of car production plants found in many of the more mature economic marketplaces in the world. In this instance, alignment between 'what could be' and the prevailing mental models of 'what was' must become highly influential elements of the new way of strategic thinking at Ford.

- **Actions and values: Facebook's "monthly active people" program:** An example of alignment touch points here are those between Facebook's North Star (Kuchler, 2019) and its organisational values. A North Star is described by Kuchler (2019) as "the strategically focused, but single metric that everyone in the company is thinking about; and ways to move that metric up". It is apparent that the North Star metric that was used at Facebook was one designed to drive extremely ambitious growth targets. An unintended outcome from its instigation, however, was that it curtailed other metrics relating to organisational values. This apparent misalignment resulted in a staggering $5 billion fine (Murphy, 2019). The fine was imposed after it was found that Facebook "had allowed users' personal data to be improperly accessed by a political targeting firm Cambridge Analytica, which was active in the 2016 US presidential election".

Not all issues of misalignment are as conceptual as the foregoing examples. Many of them relate to the more visible notions of misalignment that exist between the firm and its external environment and/or the internal operations of the firm. Some of these issues were discussed in our review of 'the impact of external forces on strategy' in Chapter 2. The impact of alignment touch points at the two Outside In external levels and the single, Inside Out internal level that were referred to previously. They are discussed next.

Level 1: Outside In, external, indirect alignment (many to many): These are the Outside In–oriented touch points that can be found between the external environment in general and the internal operations of the firm. Touch points in this category are consistent with the PESTE analysis commonly used as an input to the development of a scenario analysis. An example is US-based telecoms giant T-Mobile and its attempt to acquire rival Sprint for $26 billion.

As reported by Shubber (2019), each company thought that greater alignment between the merged firm and the consumer would offer significant benefits. These would be measured by better service, lower cost and greater reach. Indirect influencers in the form of industry regulators, however, had other ideas. When seeking to consolidate the resource base of each, T-Mobile's ambition to acquire Sprint faced objections from ten attorneys general in the US while representing their respective state governments. Their fear was that the merger would significantly reduce competition and thereby reduce customer service while increasing costs to consumers by "reducing the number of nationwide wireless operators to three" (Shubber, 2019).

Level 2: Outside In, external, direct alignment (many to one): Touch points in this category can be found between inputs to and outputs from corporate-specific entities and the industry and market-level external environment. Influenced by one of either an Inside Out or Outside In strategic orientation, an example is that of the UK-based book chain operator Waterstones. This company operates a specialist bookstore that combines its online operation with a physical retail chain network. Given the extent of disruption to the book industry following the arrival of online retailing, brick-and-mortar oriented Waterstones has done exceedingly well to not only survive but also emerge in mid-2019 as the new owner of the US bookstore chain Barnes and Noble. Having committed $683 million to the acquisition, Waterstones is expressing a great deal of confidence that it can continue to benefit from the alignment it enjoys between its virtual online customers and its face-to-face customers. This alignment describes a relationship between a commodity-based, price conscious but global online network with an equally price conscious but differentiated local and thereby limited network of in-store customers.

Level 3: Inside Out, internal alignment (one to one): It is at this level that a broad-based description of alignment can be likened to the differences between such things as actual vs. budget expenditure, planned for outcomes vs. the reality of actual outcomes or more pertinently "the difference between desired strategic objectives and realised strategic objectives". These latter differences can be found where elements and subsystems located within the Third Wave Strategy framework interact with each other.

Examples here include the fundamental and timeless issue of alignment between Strategy Evaluation, Shaping and implementation. Another is the time-honoured challenge referred to previously, that of corporate strategy vs. business unit strategy. Another is department-level strategy (human resources, finance and accounting) vs. business unit or even corporate-level strategy.

Strategic Alignment touch points in the context of Third Wave Strategy

From our experience in dealing with the issue of alignment within each of these three touch points, it has become clear that a primary cause for concern is not just the fact that a lack of alignment exists and unintended consequences arise. Rather, it is a lack of consciousness and sometimes a pure lack of awareness of the disconnect (as proposed by Trevor and Varcoe (2016)) between the most important alignment of all which, according to Ansoff (1965), is

> *the issue of alignment between an intended organisational purpose and the reality of actual outcomes that are sometimes inconsistent with purpose.*

Areas of plausible alignment touch points can be found in every business and organisation (although more obviously and potentially consequential in corporations). Their existence can also be found to be the cause of unexpected incidences and consequences, intended or otherwise, that will inevitably emerge when least expected – no matter if the business is in its early or mature stages of development.

For corporations in their early growth stage, the issue of Strategic Alignment is quite simple. At a time when emergent strategy is at its strongest, the business either succeeds in its strategic goals and objectives or it doesn't. In the case of mature and established organisations, the complexity of Alignment and consequences of a lack thereof can be significantly greater. As the years go by, there is a risk that stakeholders will consciously or subconsciously succumb to the state of Inertia that was illustrated and discussed at length through our review of the sponse matrix (Figure 1.2) and the notion of a strategic drift (Chapter 4). When considering the consequences for a corporation facing these circumstances, it has long been our belief that in most cases, the difference between *desired strategic objectives* and *realised strategic objectives* have, to say the least, become obscured.

By addressing alignment within the context of each touch point, insight into the issues are provided, as is the basis for its management by the strategy practitioner. Issues and characteristics of each touch point are discussed next. To help structure your thinking, Case example 5.1 is included here to provide context in the form of an extended case study of the Ford Motor Company. In this second review of Ford (refer Chapter 3 for the first one), the focus is placed on their need to seek realignment at each of the three touch points discussed previously. As suggested in their 2018 annual report, the Ford board of directors has defined a new purpose, a new business format and a new perspective on the way it intends to align its operations with the external environment. This case study points to the significant alignment touch points that are at play and must be adhered to in order to keep Ford on track in its newly defined journey to the future.

Case example 5.1   Journey to the future: obtaining Alignment under intensive competitive and industry pressure at Ford Motor Company

When Jim Hackett was appointed president of the Ford Motor Company in May 2018, his first objective was to address the obvious lack of alignment between its prevailing way of doing business and the potential of alternative ways that could be adopted, given the opportunity to do so. Even when industry disruptor Tesla reached higher market capitalisation than Ford, for example, the leadership team was seemingly slow to address the emerging demand for electric powered vehicles. Not to mention the adoption of the broader-based aspects of advanced 'mobility' capabilities, such as autonomous driving, car and ride sharing, and Internet-enabled augmentation of entertainment and car management systems.

Ford's problems didn't stop there though. Under newly elected US President Donald Trump, new pressure was brought to bear on the likes of Ford, Apple and Nike to reverse their decision taken years ago to locate manufacturing production facilities offshore. These decisions, Trump reasoned, were made at the expense of employment opportunities for localised American wage earners. At the same time, Ford was feeling social pressure to improve the negative impact of the release of carbon emissions into the atmosphere.

Similarly, Ford felt continued competitive pressure from lower cost and better-quality incumbents operating out of Europe, Asia and, increasingly, China. All this while demand for passenger cars continued a downward spiral and, in its place, an uptake in demand for SUVs; both circumstances had made it very hard for Ford to make any profits at all out of passenger vehicle sales.

Rather than playing catch up, newly appointed CEO Hackett opted to leapfrog the immediate head winds with a move to adopt prosponsive strategy options. Driven by an ambition to transform to a 'mobility' business (Ford Annual Report, 2017). Hackett evolved Ford's new Strategic Intent. It required Ford to make the decision to untangle past embedded alignment touch points and to reframe and break down a prevalence of destructive prevailing mental models, an example of which is provided by a Ford employee who declared, "I can't get an autonomous vacuum cleaner to find its way around my son's bedroom never mind get a car to navigate itself". Instead, Hackett proposed the company "reconnect the dots that hard wired Ford to the prosponsive adoption of a new ways to deliver its mission of 'making people's lives better by making mobility accessible and affordable'". Examples of the high-level, Strategic Alignment touch points can be found at each juncture of Ford's reinvigorated strategy. They are discussed as follows.

Level 1: Outside In, external, indirect alignment (many to many)

Throwing caution and history to the wind, and informed by a rewiring of alignment touch points, Hackett sought to realign its resource base to the demands of the emerging market for personal transportation. In accepting the inevitability of a future that looked a lot different than the past, Hackett announced (Ford Annual Report, 2018) a newly defined statement of purpose: "To become the world's most trusted company, designing smart vehicles for a smart world".

Level 2: Outside In, external direct alignment (many to one)

Realising the need to adapt to the changing face of the automotive industry as a result of automation, electrification and digitalisation, Ford elected to close many of its international manufacturing and assembly plants in the late 2010s. Such an action is a perfect example of the harsh reality of the need to identify and take notice of (re or prosponsive) the alignment touch points that may exist between the business and its environment and also between strategy and operations.

As suggested in their 2018 annual report, Ford was adopting a new approach to business and a new perspective on how it would obtain alignment with the external environment. The following, points to the significant alignment touch points that are at play and must be adhered to in order to keep Ford on track in its newly defined journey to the future. It is based on four objectives that act as drivers of strategic change. Each represent alignment touch points that must be acknowledged in order for Ford to reinvent and renew. They are as follows:

Objective	Alignment Touch Points
Create a fresher, more targeted vehicle portfolio that can compete and win in all markets where we have a presence.	Market share: Product range offered by Ford and competitor product range
Execute a compelling plan for vehicle propulsion that delights our customers and supports our commitment to reduce CO_2 emissions as part of the Paris Accord.	Car persona: The maintenance of exhilaration and fun vs. boring and responsible carbon emissions
Develop the technology, user experience and business formats to unlock the massive potential of autonomous vehicles.	Purpose of technology: The standard at which users can understand, operate and control technology over those that are beyond human control
Create a portfolio of successful mobility offerings that can deliver recurring revenue.	Dynamic Market System: Design of mobility value-based market system and retention of the customer base

Level 3: Inside Out, internal alignment (one to one) with strategy

What is Ford going to do to continue to realign operations with strategy? According to their 2018 Annual Report Ford is: "Looking to improve returns in the nearer term by reducing costs, improving operating efficiencies and focusing resources on vehicles that better meet our customers' needs". These are listed below in the context of the areas and 'sub areas' of plausible touch points:

- **Operations, resources:** shifting 90 percent of our North American vehicle line up volume to sport utility vehicles, crossovers, trucks and commercial vehicles between 2018 and the end of 2020.
- **Operations, product range:** refreshing 75 percent of our line up in the United States by the end of 2020.
- **Governance, social responsibility:** committing to reducing vehicle emissions by delivering CO_2 reductions consistent with the Paris Accord.
- **Operations, modernisation:** investing $11 billion in electrification, and plan to electrify our most popular nameplates, including an all-electric Mustang-inspired performance utility and Ford F-150.

In Ford's case, there was apparently no acknowledgement of highly evident, historical but external information that pointed to the emergence of the amorphous mass of new technology that had been under development for quite some time. A key factor essentially missed by Ford was the dramatic increase in demand for electric-powered vehicles, so large was this apparent opportunity, it propelled deliberately disruptive and industry rival Tesla to outperform Ford, even though Ford remained one of the long term industry incumbents. As described in Case example 5.1, newly appointed CEO Jim Hackett moved to realign Ford's strategic posturing through strategies of Deliberate Disruption. The task he faced in initiating and sustaining a program of transformation, however, was vast compared to what might have been had they commenced only a few years prior.

Similar to Fords experience, first and second wave strategy practitioners are used to experiencing a lack of alignment on a regular basis and in situations where some experiences are a lot more significant than others. The occurrences and consequences of such experiences were discussed at length in Chapter 2. There we assessed the impact of external forces on corporate-level strategy. The reason for its return in this chapter is the fact that it is dedicated specifically to a discussion of plausable alignment touch points and their influence on the often unseen 'forces that prevail'. The concept of plausable touch points at each of the three different levels of alignment are discussed next.

Level 1: Outside In, external indirect alignment (many to many): Plausible touch points between the internal strategy system and the universal, external environment in general (economic, industry, markets, stakeholder influences).

As discussed in Chapters 3 and 4, and as illustrated in Figure 5.2, the conduct of Strategic Alignment in the context of the high-level, broad-based external environment is addressed in two ways. First is its treatment as a part of a Strategy Evaluation, Shaping program. Here we have demonstrated in some detail the value of in-depth environmental scanning regime. It includes first of all assessments of Five Forces analysis, PESTE analysis and scenario analysis. Second is the ongoing maintenance and management of alignment which can be included as an instrumental component of a broad-based Strategy Evaluation renewal exercise (Chapter 3). This was also discussed specifically as a component of the Program of Continual Strategy Renewal in Chapter 4 (Figure 4.1). There, your attention was drawn to the strategy-focused performance, measurement, management, monitoring and reporting mechanism, which is a component of the broader construct of the Program of Continual Strategy Renewal. As suggested in Chapters 3 and 4 also, Strategy Evaluation in itself is a knowledge-based component of the strategy monitoring mechanism. It consciously prompts for the evaluation and revaluation of assumptions, intuitive judgements, guestimates and estimates that are prone to a loss of relevance over time. It is recommended that these are included in the monitoring of changes in the broad-based external environment that may lead to a lack of alignment and associated, unintended consequences: good or bad.

Touch Points	External Areas and 'Sub-areas' of Plausible Touch Points
Level 1. Outside in external, indirect alignment: *Long Term Strategy*	• Political, economic, social, technological, ecological (PESTE) • Porter's Five Forces of Industry Attractiveness

Figure 5.2 A depiction of external, indirect areas where possible alignment touch points may be found of relevance to all strategy timelines (short, medium and long)

Level 2: Outside In, external direct alignment (many to one): Plausible touch points between inputs to and outputs from corporate-specific entities and the industry and market-level external environment.

In this second level of plausible touch points of Strategic Alignment (illustrated as Figure 5.3), our analysis is based on the observation that much of corporate strategy is concerned with the issue of corporate *configuration*. According to Meyer (2007), for example, corporate-level strategy is about determining the

Touch Points	External Areas and 'Sub-areas' of Plausible Touch Points		
Level 2. Outside In, external, direct alignment: *Medium term development projects*	Outside In	Networks, alliances, international/global expansion	Mergers and acquisitions (M&A)
	Inside Out	Corporate structuring and diversification	

Figure 5.3 A depiction of external, direct areas where possible alignment touch points may be found

configuration that offers 'best of both world' solutions to the tension between the dichotomies of a focus on the following:

Customer responsiveness: A structure that focuses on a distributed resource base that is intended to endear customer relationships. An example is a luxurious five-star hotel.

Synergy: An emphasis on the optimisation of firm resources and a more standardised approach to customer relationships, an example is a budget, two-star hotel chain.

Naturally, it is recommended that the impact of re and prosponsive change is considered when assessing positive attributes in the corporate configuration process. It is proposed therefore, that

> *re and pro sponsiveness in corporate strategy effectiveness is defined as "the ability to either adapt to or invent answers to the competitive demands of a specific business area in a timely and adequate manner".*

This reference according to Meyer (2007) refers to a firm's capacity or, indeed, choice to focus primarily on the customer as opposed to the cost of satisfying customer needs, which is the domain of synergy.

> *Synergy is the additional value created by working in two or more business areas, over and above the sum of the business parts.*

Here a corporation is choosing to focus on the optimisation of firm resources (primarily through the minimisation of operational costs) as opposed to focusing on the prioritisation of customers' every need. It could be said that the former is complementary to a focus on an Outside In strategy. The latter (synergy) is a complementary focus on an Inside Out strategy.

Inside Out vs. Outside In sources of alignment

As illustrated in Figure 5.3, a corporation's interaction with the external environment can occur from either an Outside In or Inside Out point of view. Inevitably, solutions from either perspective will contribute to decisions concerning a corporation's strategy in the medium term. The term 'medium' term strategy is used deliberately, as it is our view that the analysis and implementation of opportunity through the mechanisms identified in Figure 5.3 will inevitably take longer than Short Term Strategy but not as long as Long Term Strategy. Medium term strategy requires deep research and detailed, complex analysis before conclusions can be reached and a decision made. In the development of medium term strategy, an appreciation of the implications of adopting an Outside In and/or an Inside Out approach will enable a smoother outcome and understanding/appreciation of alignment.

Outside In perspective

From this perspective, medium term strategy practice will provide insight into the question of alignment that was first proposed by Ansoff. It is the leveraging of resources into an environment which is concerned with the "selection of the product mix which the firm will produce and the markets to which it will sell?" Put another way, it is "deciding what business the firm is in and what kinds of business it will seek to enter?" (Ansoff, 1965). In this context, practitioners must address how to optimise any opportunities that may be found through the corporation's involvement in the formation of networks with other corporations and related businesses. Such analysis should also include the formation of formal partnerships and/or alliances and expansion into international and potentially global markets.

The clear message here is that in any aspect of network building, alliance forming and so on, the issue of alignment must be identified and addressed. Suffice to say, it is our opinion that

> *the realisation of a positive alignment with potential alliance partners, mergers and acquisition targets, international and national networks is a key priority, second only to the requisite for positive financial return.*

Seeking an opportunity for growth in the automotive sector in 1988, for example, leaders of both the highly operations-focused Inside Out–oriented Mercedes Benz and the highly marketing-oriented Outside In–focused Chrysler were happy that theirs would be a merger of equals. Although this may have been the case at a conceptual level, speculation was rife at the time of the announcement that the cultures of each firm would never be reconciled – or aligned. Regrettably, the pundits were right, and the alliance collapsed. After a mere nine years, the $36 billion 'merger of equals' was dissolved when Cerberus Capital Management took an 80.1% stake in Chrysler for a paltry sum of $7.4 billion (Mateja, 2007).

Inside Out perspective

From this perspective, Ansoff (1965) observed that the "the objective (of strategy) is to produce a resource allocation pattern which will offer the best potential for meeting the firm's objectives". Opportunities to extend the resource base could become available from diversification, engagement in M&A activities or both. Keeping in mind the fact that Ansoff developed these thoughts in a static, predictive environment, however, the practitioner should be aware that it is unlikely that this approach will hold much weight in the complex and uncertain business world that we inhabit today. In an environment of Third Wave Strategy, especially, it is necessary to continue to review, renew and, in many instances, continually evolve the resource base in order to satisfy the never-ending changes in market demand for the corporation's goods and services.

Perhaps one of the most important aspects of Alignment now becomes apparent as we refer again to our adaptation of Chandler's observation that "after purpose is established, a strategy is evolved. Structure then follows strategy and systems follow structure". What makes this observation so important is the fact that just as strategy is dynamic and must be constantly reviewed and renewed, so must the resource base – and by definition the associated organisation structure, processes and systems – be constantly reviewed and renewed. To emphasise this point, and in a final response to Trevor and Varcoe's (2016) previous comments it can now be concluded that

> *just as strategy must be "flexed and changed" in response to exponential forces impacting the internal and external environment, so too must organisational structures, systems and processes flex and change to reflect the ebb and flow of changes in strategy.*

Regeneration as an antidote to poor Alignment

A recognition of the need for organisational structures to flex and change to reflect the ebb and flow of dynamic strategy practices lies in stark contrast to most prevailing organisational restructuring activities. As discussed in Chapter 4, most change events are undertaken in a one-off stepped tranche of unfreeze–change–refreeze (Lewin, 1947). Perhaps an alternative to this decidedly non-nimble approach to change should now be considered. As an idea that was also discussed in Chapter 4, it can now be concluded that:

> *Regeneration is enacted within the context of deliberate 'tweaking' of resources in the form of a continual alignment and realignment rather than a state of panic.*

As discussed in Chapter 4 also, the rapid redeployment of resources is one of three key aspects of Doz and Kosonen's (2008) approach to Agile Strategy practice. Referring to this capability as *resource fluidity*, the authors observe,

> *This phenomenon refers to a leadership's internal capability to seamlessly "reconfigure capabilities and to rapidly redeploy resources".*

The implications for organisational stability are significant as organisational culture is built around certainty and predictability. The promise of such conditions will soon be increasingly harder to justify. As an example of the immediacy of this situation, Third Wave Strategy practitioner Amazon has already recognised the need to manage rapid restructuring and by association the continual transformation of its structure. In order to defend itself against the inevitable disruption created by ongoing transformation, Amazon has announced plans to help its workers gain new skills. As reported by the *Wall Street Journal* (Cutter, 2019), for example, Amazon will "spend $700 million over about six years to retrain a third of its U.S.

workforce as automation, machine learning and other technology upends the way many of its employees do their jobs". Amazon isn't alone in its recognition of this need. Other companies undertaking similar activities, according to the *Wall Street Journal*, are AT&T, Walmart, JPMorgan Chase & Co. and Accenture.

Should the opportunity for either be sought or unexpectedly arise, such an eventuality could well be of interest to the strategy practitioner from both an Inside Out and Outside In strategic positioning perspective. By way of illustration, GE Energy found not long after its acquisition of French-based energy company Alstom in 2015 that an appropriate alignment between expected outcomes and realised outcomes can become unaligned very apparently and very quickly. A brief description of the GE/Alstom experience exemplifies how hard acquisitions can be and how lessons must be learned. The case is explored in Case example 5.2.

Case example 5.2   Lessons from obtaining Alignment in GE's acquisition of Alstom

GE Power makes and services large-scale turbines that are deployed in the use of electricity generation. Seeking a break from continued investment in oil and gas, GE embarked on an acquisition worth $10.6 billion that saw them acquire French company Alstom's power and grid unit. It is a good example of the way in which corporate strategy can stray from business unit strategy and as an outcome impose unintended consequences on firm performance.

At the time of the acquisition, according to Patel (2017), cracks were already starting to appear in the GE oil and gas division's operating performance. In the November 2017 investor call, for example, Patel (2017) observed that CEO John Flannery lamented, "While the GE Power franchise remained 'good', even in the face of a 'tough market', GE had 'exacerbated the market situation with some really poor execution'". At the same time, energy prices had collapsed and demand for oil field services of the type that GE provided were dropping rapidly.

GE's power unit was the company's largest in terms of revenue; its overall profit margin of 19.4% was one of the highest in the company. Sales were expanding up to 11% in 2014, making an expansion of the power division a reasonable thing to do. The problems with this strategy were, however, numerous, according to Colvin (2018). In preparing their bid for Alstom, the GE acquisition swat team knew that profit margins were less than par, but the GE team mistakenly believed it could raise them, Colvin (2018) continued. Another assumption the GE team made also turned out to be incorrect. Rather than generating cash by selling the advisory services, division regulators made them divest Alstom's service business in order to let it pass. Instead of reducing costs, therefore, the acquisition added more than 30,000 additional salaries to the operating cost base. "Still", Colvin noted, "GE thought they could more than pay for themselves".

Regrettably, the worst was yet to come. Just as GE made this huge investment in fossil-fuelled power generation that was the hallmark of Alstom's operations, wind, solar and other forms of renewable energy sources were starting to come on stream and, accordingly, would be more cost competitive than in the past. This made it difficult to clawback the extra overheads GE had incurred through the acquisition, requiring them instead to carry them right thorough to the bottom line. As a result, Colvin duly noted, "Global demand for GE Power's products collapsed, and profit plunged 45% – GE is still trying to recover".

The lessons to be learned from the identification of specific alignment touch points is to capture those incidences and to never forget them. This is, of course, a case of organisational learning on the go. In many cases, the task of identifying and completing mergers and acquisitions, the conduct of diversification and even the structuring of organisations, as well as the development of a global strategy, are often undertaken independently of the mainstream corporate strategy practitioners. This creates barriers between the function of Strategy Evaluation, Shaping and implementation and a corporate-wide disconnect that makes overall synchronisation difficult to maintain. To illustrate,

> *for many companies, an acquisition team can often be working in isolation to the CSO's team. Charged with the mission to identify and implement "bolt on acquisitions", the results of each team's independent work can be counterproductive or plain destructive.*

Others are just challenging in logic, as demonstrated in the GE/Alstom case.

Resolving conflict of Alignment with the external environment

In many ways, the measurement, management, monitoring and reporting of disconnected touch points can be treated as an extension of the Program of Continual Strategy Renewal (Figure 4.2). This, in turn, you will recall is an embedded and integral component of the firm's performance measurement, management, monitoring and reporting mechanism. Specifically, it is suggested that the formal reporting mechanism is enhanced to include matters of alignment and nonalignment, assessed as measures of strategic risk. Reporting of risk in this construct could include the potential for the onset of unintended consequences to occur or not.

As demonstrated in Figure 5.4, colour coding can be used to highlight differences between those carrying high, medium or low risk profiles.

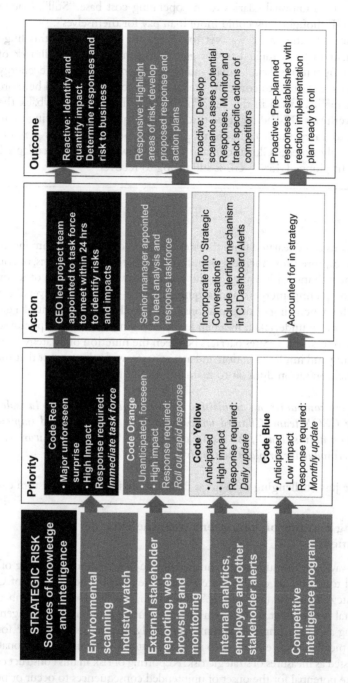

Figure 5.4 A monitoring and reporting mechanism enabling the management of strategic risk

Level 3: Inside Out, internal alignment (one to one): Plausible touch points within the system itself, that is the internal, core components of the system that interact with each other.

In Figure 5.5 plausible alignment touch points of relevance to the internal operations of the business are illustrated. In this context, we have explored the need for internal alignment at various stages of this book. Similarly, we have alerted you to the need for alignment between operations and strategy. The realisation of alignment in this context, however, will be different for each organisation. To provide an illustration and confirmation of this, you are invited to compare the approach to alignment adopted by Jim Hackett at Ford (Case example 5.1) with the approach adopted by Jeff Bezos at Amazon (Case example 5.3).

As Ford CEO, Jim Hackett had the task of reinventing a corporation that was very set in its ways. Radical, disruptive change was required to both maintain and leapfrog change in its industry and markets. At the same time, it was deemed necessary to revolutionise the Ford leadership as the incumbent team seemed to be ensconced in a world of denial, disinterest and disconnect with reality. In contrast, it is useful to recognise the differences in the nature of internal alignment that can be found within Amazon. It is one that demonstrates how a source of a renewable competitive advantage can be turned into a customer-centric Dynamic Market System (refer to Chapter 2). Success at Amazon under Bezos's leadership shows that although there have been a number of failures, there have also been many successes. Failures include the Amazon Fire mobile phone. Successes include Amazon Prime, Cloud Computing and Alexa. Each of the latter products have excelled, thereby supporting the continued growth of a deliberately disruptive, emergent corporation. To succeed, Bezos has followed a philosophy of creating a fear of failure as a means of avoiding Amazon falling

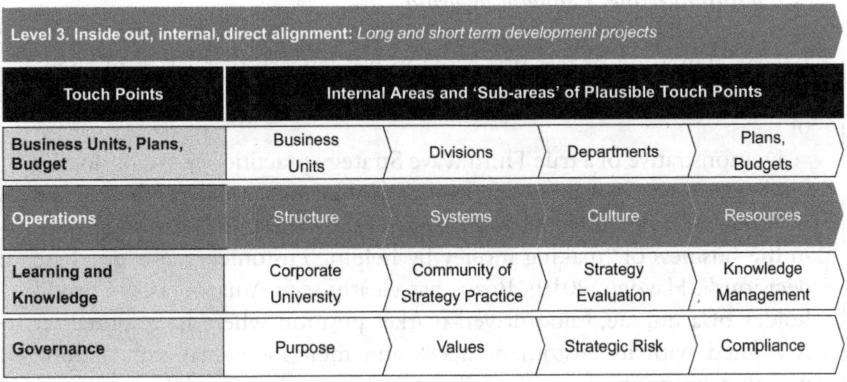

Level 3. Inside out, internal, direct alignment: *Long and short term development projects*				
Touch Points	**Internal Areas and 'Sub-areas' of Plausible Touch Points**			
Business Units, Plans, Budget	Business Units	Divisions	Departments	Plans, Budgets
Operations	Structure	Systems	Culture	Resources
Learning and Knowledge	Corporate University	Community of Strategy Practice	Strategy Evaluation	Knowledge Management
Governance	Purpose	Values	Strategic Risk	Compliance

Figure 5.5 A depiction of internal areas where possible alignment touch points may be found of relevance mostly to Short Term Strategy timelines

into the state of stasis that Ford found itself in. Bezos achieved this in no small way by ensuring that

> *Amazon remained a Day 1 company; that is, a company that exists in a permanent state of renewal amidst a constant state of paranoia.*

An exploration of the notion of paranoia at Amazon is discussed in the context of alignment in Case example 5.3.

Case example 5.3   Seeking perfect Alignment and organisational structuring at Amazon

There is no better example of the integrated nature of purpose-driven Alignment than Amazon, whose CEO and founder, Jeff Bezos, is entirely consumed by the notion of aligning strategy with customer centricity. To this day, Bezos continues to apply the ethos of a start-up company by consistently reminding employees and all stakeholders of the words he expressed in his original 1977 letter to shareholders. There, he described how passionately he believed that Amazon should remain a 'day one company'. Consistent with the idea once proposed by Andy Grove (1999) when he was CEO of Intel, "only the paranoid survive", Bezos consistently reminds everyone at Amazon that it will always be a day one company. That is one that's always hustling, always focused, Bezos suggested. As Bariso (2017) has reported, Bezos's response to an employee who bravely asked him what 'day two' looks like, his comment was from the dark side:

> *Day two is stasis. Followed by irrelevance. Followed by excruciating, painful decline. Followed by death.*

Bezos's expression of fear was based in his concern that a lack of alignment between the firm and its customers' desires would lead to this state of stasis.

Demonstrative of a true Third Wave Strategy practitioner, Bezos doesn't see Amazon simply as an online retailer. Unlike most retailers whose ethos is simply to keep costs low and margins high, Amazon, Bezos suggests is in the business of "making money by helping customers make purchase decisions" (Hayden, 2019). Bezos has clearly seen Amazon as the proud holder of a unique, value-driven market position where its resource set is aligned with its customers' needs and their individual expectations; its value proposition is informing customers as opposed to managing transactions.

Bezos is not overly concerned with what would-be competitors are doing. In an interview with Kirby and Stewart from the *Harvard Business Review*, Bezos stressed that to become the most efficient online retailer in the world, he has been more concerned with the voice of the customer than anything or anyone else. "If you're competitor focused, you tend to slack off when your benchmarks say that you're the best. But if your focus is on customers, you keep improving" (Lane, 2018).

Amazon's value system orientation is visible in one sense, that of the position of adjacency. This position becomes apparent through the obvious capacity for Amazon to expand into other industries and markets that are close to the business areas where it already holds powerful positions. As an example, Amazon has broken new ground in industry ethos. It is true, for example, that the retail industry has struggled significantly over the years. By focusing solely on the realisation of small profit margins obtained by buying low and selling high, few have been able to offer a differentiated value proposition greater than that offered by Amazon.

Now an operator of significant power in the buying, moving and distribution and delivery of retail items, Amazon is able to move vertically, horizontally or in any direction it chooses. The most recent example of the way in which Amazon's customer focus and adjacency solutions combine to propel its growth is the uptake of its music streaming service. "The number of people subscribing to Amazon Music Unlimited has grown by about 70 per cent in 2019" (Nicolaou, 2019). In contrast, according to Nicolaou, "Spotify, the world's largest streaming service with 100m subscribers, is growing at about 25 per cent a year".

As the notion of a an Integrated Value System in product and service design is not yet a conscious business format, it will be one day. No doubt, the notion will become apparent to Bezos anyway – at the point where the borders of adjacency align and the realisation of a value system (Chapter 2) emerges.

It is this Level 3 Inside Out internal form of alignment that is the easiest to control. That is because most of the issues creating misalignment are readily visible. Most of the issues of relevance are also well within the purview of the firm's leadership.

6 Future strategy practice

Thematic setting: *Future focused strategy and corporate practices*

Introduction: building momentum

We have learned a great detail about the concept of Third Wave Strategy and the transformation of organisations in the previous chapters of this book. Our primary objective has been to identify a range of alternative strategy practices that you may follow, depending on your circumstances, ambitions, resources and capabilities. Of all these strategies, Deliberate Disruption could appear to be the most challenging option. At the same time, however, it is also the one that should be adopted if an organisation is to continually evolve in the context of a Hyper – HPO.

The journey explored in this book commenced in earnest in the mid-1960s following the 'lighting of the fuse' by Igor Ansoff in 1965. Ansoff provided the foundation for the conduct of first wave, static strategic planning. As our story of enhancement unfolded, so did our own structure for strategy. What we ended up with is considerably more dynamic than our starting position. Take the Strategic Architecture as an example. As a result of remastering our perception of Long Term Strategy from a simplistic Inside Out, Outside In model of Long Term Strategy, it evolved into a depiction of a dynamic Integrated Value System. An illustration of a Strategic Architecture of relevance to Amazon and more attuned to the picture that was painted as a result of our remastering appears in Figure 6.1. You will note that the activities of procuring and producing, as well as recycling have been added to the Dynamic Market System design. This was done to emphasise the fact that as a system, there is always a pre-processing and post-processing component to be included. It signifies, therefore, the need for corporations to recognise the need to incorporate both elements into their system design. It is only through this recognition that the service offering can be recognised as a fully integrated service solution. Although potentially higher cost, the offset to that is the fact that the recycling component especially is not going to be a particularly attractive task for the customer either. They may, therefore, be prepared to pay extra for that service offering.

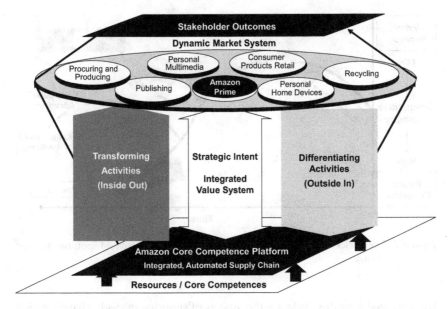

Figure 6.1 A perspective of the dynamic Strategic Architecture at Amazon

The content of this book has so far has been concerned with the transformation of a single entity moving towards the Utopian position of regeneration and Hyper – High Performance. The Ford case provided insight into a notion of ambidextrousness as it sought to transform from a car company to a mobility company. The question is, what if this is not enough? What if it wanted to evolve a series of unrelated businesses out of the core business? As discussed, Amazon grew a billion-dollar cloud computing platform out of a retail company, and Apple is mid-way through its development of an entertainment company out of its still profitable computer company. Could Ford do the same? The answer is yes; it is also a viable option for any business that adopts the concept that was also referred to in previous chapters: the notion of Green Shoot Strategy. The appeal of the Green Shoot Strategy is its promise of developing new businesses entirely out of the continually healthy and sustainable core, potentially a new industry altogether. We explore the capacity to evolve a Green Shoot Strategy next.

Sprouting a clean, fresh, new opportunity: Green Shoot Strategy and accelerated Deliberate Disruption

The context for the evolution of a Green Shoot Strategy is presented in Figure 6.2. In this diagram, you will observe the illustration of outcomes from a traditional business trajectory travailed by a product, service or an entire business.

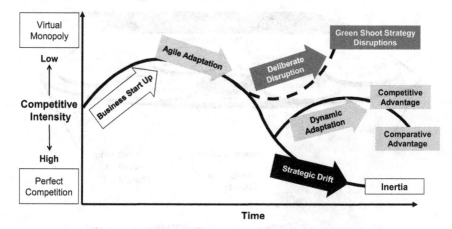

Figure 6.2 Life cycles of businesses engaging in the four perspective of sponsive strategic change

Incorporated into this cycle are the aspects of sponsive strategic change which were first presented and illustrated in Figure 1.2.

If you assume the life cycle illustrated in Figure 6.2 is that of a business, you can readily observe in the middle of the diagram a well-trodden trajectory. It commences with a successful and joyous launch. Success is always dependent on its capacity to avoid competitors that come up with a better solution. Inevitably they will, so at some point, this company will be forced into a debilitating strategic drift. Examples are the pioneers of the mobile phone industry, Nokia and Black Berry. Each were industry leaders in the mobile phone space before being crushed by Apple. Should a firm seek to avoid or evolve from this circumstance, it may choose to engage in a more prosponsive activity of restructuring.

As an Agile, or even Dynamic, Adapter, an improvement in performance could be realised as a result of the breakaway from the natural decline of the original business. This adaptative or inventive diversification starts out positively, but it too will most likely be limited to the realisation of a short term competitive advantage at best, a commodity oriented comparative advantage at worst. We contend however that a state of regeneration realised through the invention of an incontestable Green Shoot opportunity offers the greatest potential in the long term. It is shown on the upper-right side of the diagram.

Born out of core business, but in a different or breakaway format, a Green Shoot Strategy is derived out of an accelerated form of Deliberate Disruption. It is given this name because it reflects the green shoots of a plant or tree, the establishment of a greenfield manufacturing facility or an economic recovery. Accelerated disruption occurs once a prosponsively driven invention has demonstrated a mutation. A mutation is an event that is a natural occurrence for a *living system* (Parent, 2000) or, in the context of an organisation, a *living company* (de Gues, 1997). We have previously attributed the notion of a 'living company' to Arie de Gues, who applied it to his notion of a 'learning organisation'. De Gues linked strategy to learning through his observation first quoted in Chapter 3: It is "the speed of learning may be a firm's only real source of sustainable competitive advantage". Unlike a living organism, a living company has the capacity to not only adapt but also to invent and thereby evolve new business entities altogether. The occurrence of such an evolutionary event is referred to as a Green Shoot Strategy mutation. This mutation is confirmed when a business demonstrates a capacity to deliver a breakaway opportunity through the realisation of a single discontinuity or series of multiple discontinuities.

A discontinuity is said to occur when a Green Shoot, accelerated Deliberate Disruption emerges from the act of multidextrous opportunity seeking. To be sustainable, it must separate from the core business and continue to survive and thrive on its own. Examples of such breakaways are numerous. One standout practitioner of Green Shoot Strategy is Virgin Group, established and led by serial entrepreneur Richard Branson, as discussed in Case example 6.1.

Case example 6.1 Virgin Group: serendipitous opportunity or adaptation of an Integrated Value System?

In the early 1970s, Richard Branson, founder and owner of Virgin Group, established a mail order record distribution business from a London flat. In 1972, he went on to found the Virgin Records music label, signing stars such as Genesis, the Sex Pistols and the Rolling Stones. In 2013, Branson credited the £500 million pound sale of Virgin Records as the basis upon which the company could fund its investment in the broad-based portfolio that it has on full display today. Branson described his interest in life as "setting huge, apparently unachievable challenges and trying to rise above them" (Economy, 2015).

Virgin Group is described on its website as "a family owned growth capital investor, with a globally recognised and respected brand". Virgin's aim is to deliver long term capital appreciation through investment in five sectors of travel and leisure, telecoms and media, music and entertainment, financial services and health and wellness. Virgin is also an active technology-focused venture investor. It has a portfolio of over 35 companies spanning the consumer, Internet, fintech and sharing economy sectors.

Although characteristic of a global conglomerate, Virgin has built a Core Competence Platform, which they suggest (indirectly) consists of

- sector expertise and track record across the five core sectors mentioned previously;
- experience and understanding of consumer behaviour, brands and marketing; and
- a strong network of investors, management teams and alumni.

At the group level, Virgin doesn't have a Dynamic Market System *per se*; what it does have is a traditional portfolio of independent business units that are categorised by resource type. The space strategic business unit, for example, consists of space travel business unit Virgin Galactic and satellite launch business unit Globe. The basis for a Dynamic Market System that could emerge from a collation of Virgin business units clustered around an emergent Dynamic Market System could be travel related. With a travel agency booking platform established as a Core Competence Platform, a Dynamic Market System could be evolved from a Virgin-owned collaborative of Virgin-branded space travel options, airlines, trains, resorts, hotels and cruises.

An accelerated Deliberate Disruption is similar in nature to a mutated open system. As a living system, a company can be likened to natural biological entities, such as forests, rivers and rainforests. An example of a Green Shoot Disruption emerging within the context of a natural living system is a lake that features outcrops of ferns and reeds on its banks. The origin of the lake is a discontinuity that arose from the natural redirection of a river that left an area once catastrophic floods receded, never to return. What the river did leave was an area where water could both settle and be replenished regularly. In contrast, the origin of the reeds and evolving micro-system of birds, other native plants and wild animals reflects the process of adaptation as a result of the propagation of seeds that have blown in or are dropped by birds and animals moving in from other environments.

A similar occurrence in an organisation will arise as a result of an accelerated Deliberate Disruption followed by a discontinuity of similar substance to that experienced by the lake. A living organisation, however, possess the capability to deliberately move the firm beyond the boundaries of its existing systems. In doing so,

> *the discontinuity changes the nature of competition in the industry or indeed, creates a new market or industry altogether.*

A capacity to create a new market or industry of significance size is difficult. Apple achieved it with its MacBook, iPod, iPad, iWatch, Apple TV and then Apple TV+. IKEA achieved it with its do-it-yourself furniture assembly system. Google has done it in numerous ways. We adapt the sponse matrix, therefore, to incorporate the extent and rate of change that may occur within each quadrant of the matrix, as illustrated in Figure 6.3.

Companies engaging in both *re* and *pros*ponsiveness are well positioned to create rapid large-scale disruption. As a result of advances in digital technology and changes in social norms Green Shoot accelerated Deliberate Disruptions are occurring quite often and are increasingly more likely to be born out of an Integrated Value System. A number of examples of such a system are listed in Table 2.1. Its application to Apple whose life cycle of product developments are reflected within the combined Integrated Value System and SMI Model of Strategic Equilibrium, are shown in Figure 6.4.

Apple's reliance in, and success with, its iPhone-grounded Integrated Value System has been so great that it has survived an onslaught from competitors. A key competitor is Samsung. It has adopted many key features of the Apple Value System, at least in the smartphone arena. Such is the strength of an Integrated Value System. Apple continues year after year to thrive as a Hyper − HPO. Other examples of Integrated Value Systems that have originated from an accelerated disruption of similar or same businesses include Uber, Airbnb and drive by the hour car clubs such as Go Get and Zip Car. Some Green Shoot

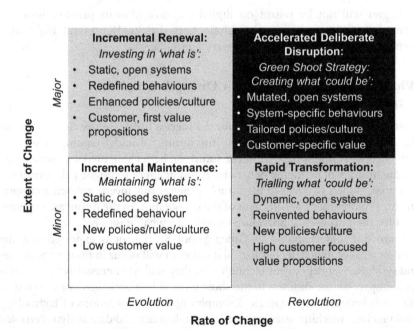

Figure 6.3 Sponse matrix adjusted to the rate and extent of change

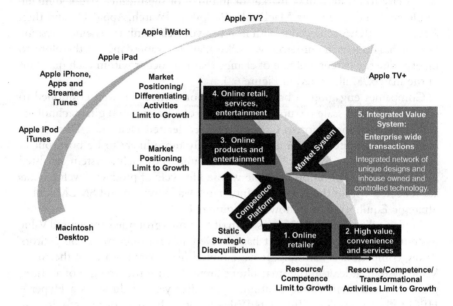

Figure 6.4 Integrated Value System within the SMI Model of Strategic Equilibrium: Apple

Strategies will not be reliant on digital technology as its primary resource. Examples of those that aren't include Lego bricks, IKEA and high-value branded goods, such as Gucci, Burberry and Tiffany's.

What might be: a Green Shoot Disruption and the corporation of the future

Those things that make an organisation a success today are not necessarily the things that will make it successful in the future. An understanding of ways to influence what might happen in the future or, better still, invent opportunities for the future will be highly beneficial. A modicum of foresight will contribute to a preparedness to adapt to the future or, better still, invent it when appropriate. An exploration of perspectives of the corporation of the future are explored next for the purposes of providing insight into what 'might be'.

From our understanding of Green Shoot Strategy, it is expected that the greatest areas of digital/technological disruption will occur in business processes and systems. As independent technologies, they will not necessarily have a strategic impact on the business in the short term. When combined, however, they may well become very strategic. Examples of these applications of technology could include machine learning, artificial intelligence and data analytics enabled by the realisation of system and process reconstruction, destruction or robotisation. The enormity of these newfound capabilities will most likely be in the areas of administration, design, manufacture, the supply chain in general and service delivery specifically. Benefits will then flow on to the conceptualisation and development of new and innovative business entities and value-based products and services that were previously thought to be difficult – or impossible – to provide. Hence the demand for Green Shoot innovative and multidextrous strategic thinking.

The corporation of the future: some perspectives

To set the scene for our appreciation of strategy practice in the future, we present a picture (Case example 6.2) of what that new future might look like, not forgetting that the major elements of that perspective are already starting to unfold. The picture we describe (Case example 6.2) represents an out of this world business environment some 30 years hence. This is a perspective of an outer-space world where life on Mars is a reality.

Case example 6.2   Intergalactic commerce 30 years into the future

It's 2050, and a colony of cyborgs (humans whose bodies are mostly flesh but also part machine) living on Mars are monitoring three-dimensional printing machines as they work towards the 'humanisation' of the planet. Their priority is to engage in environmental and industrial activities that will create the atmospheric conditions capable of supporting and sustaining human life. Other activities include the printing of interconnected dome houses, the nurturing of artificial green spaces, the assembly of mobility infrastructure and the construction of interplanetary space ports.

In this world, resident pioneers survive through decision-making processes that are enhanced with the help of augmented intelligence. Augmented intelligence is a term applied to "describe how normal human intelligence is supplemented through the pairing of people and machines" (Padmanabhan, 2018). This capability incorporates the processing of massive knowledge content, piped wirelessly to memory chips that are hardwired to human brains. Recently renamed New Mars, the plant's inhabitants are overseeing another form of mobility that is being printed and maintained. It is available in the form of light-powered space rovers, spaceships and an interconnected tubed rail system. New Mars is now an interim stop off for those connecting with the universe's interplanetary travel network. Travelling at speeds of up to 100 million miles an hour, energy that powers both tourist and industrial workhorse spaceships is derived from a ground-based laser beam that pushes ultra-light nano crafts through the emptiness of space (Breakthrough Starshot, 2017).

Back on planet Earth, high performance, 'super' corporations are now virtual entities consisting of 'space-based cloud' systems and control mechanisms. All are supported by interplanetary virtual machine learning, which in turn is enabled by earthbound and intergalactic manufacturing and supply chain networks. Each benefit from the deployment of 3D printers, smart fabrics, robotics and broad-based mobility solutions that are interconnected literally on a universal scale. Thanks to the commercialisation of quantum computers, most of the drudgery that was previously done by humans is now automated. In its place, however, humans have evolved numerous ways to intrigue and entertain themselves; they still need, though, to love, eat, sleep, achieve and explore.

There is a comprehensive range of new technologies that both make up the picture presented in Case example 6.2 and confirm that the picture is a plausible representation of that future. Content contained in Table 6.1 is a random collection of digital technological changes of relevance to all levels of external and internal alignment. Most significant amongst the technologies are the software capabilities associated with the digitalisation of just about everything. Above all, and admittedly still some years away, we refer you to Google and its recent claim to have mastered a key element of the one technology that is likely going to be the biggest technological game changer in history, that of quantum computing. Early stages of *Quantum Supremacy*, according to Google (Madhumita and Waters, 2019), have already been reached, as

[Google's] processor has performed a calculation in three minutes and 20 seconds. This is significant because the same calculation would take today's most advanced classical computer (Summit) approximately 10,000 years.

Table 6.1 Levels of alignment in an era of advanced technology

Level 1: Outside In, external, indirect and broad-based environmental touch point (many to many)

- **Quantum computing:** A revolution in computing technology that replaces the traditional Yes/No computer logic with quantum physics thereby improving processing at a much, much higher rate (Madhumita and Waters, 2019).
- **Internet of Things (IoT):** Web-based communications that connects many machines and instruments (e.g. cars, computers and appliances (amongst many other things) with each other across local, international and global boundaries.

- **5G Mobile telecommunication networks:** An enhancement to 4G technology, it provides telco users with faster connection and processing speeds and improves wide area coverage as well as high density (e.g. sport stadiums, conference facilities) access.
- **Space travel:** In addition to tourism, space travel has other commercial applications such as resource mining and even human rehabilitation services. The latter a very recent advance which included the idea that zero gravity could kill off cancer cells in human bodies (Chou, 2019).

Level 2: Outside In, external, direct alignment (many to one)

- **Blockchain:** According to Perry (2017), blockchain is "used in a peer-to-peer network of parties, who all participate in a given transaction". An example is a Bitcoin financial transaction. However, the technology is often applied to many other sources of transaction such as the sale of land, commodities and high value consumer goods.
- **Artificial intelligence:** "Machines that respond to stimulation consistent with traditional responses from humans, given the human capacity for contemplation, judgment, and intention" (Shubhendu and Vijay, 2013).
- **Augmented and virtual reality:** According to Emspak (2018), it is the "result of using technology to superimpose information – sounds, images and text – on the world we see. It adds to the reality you would ordinarily see rather than replaces it". This is different from virtual reality, which is "a computer-generated environment that allows humans to interact with, and become immersed in" (Emspak, 2018).

Level 3: Inside Out, internal alignment (one to one)

- **Machine learning:** Automated robots and other machines equipped with sensors, and Artificial Intelligence (AI) capabilities that gives them a capacity to improve the way they do the work.
- **3D and 4D printing (additive manufacturing):** Customised and remote printing of a broad range of physical objects such as machine parts, objects of art, buildings, tools and ultimately human tissues/organs.
- **Advanced materials:** Materials such as rare earths demonstrating newfound levels of strength, conductivity and functionality; some with self-healing capabilities.
- **Genomics:** Manipulate genes for health diagnostics/treatment.

What to do with all this technology?

Those pursuing the application of Third Wave Strategy practice to business are bound to experience a profound and significant impact. Conversely, those not willing to adopt its practice will no doubt be quite literally left in a state of Inertia. That's because of the significant changes that are occurring in the areas of corporate management, leadership, organisational structuring and method of operation, as well as social interaction at all levels of a corporation. Examples of changes that can be expected in the future include the following:

Corporate ownership: A transformation from public-to-private ownership: the latter becoming the new norm, especially as corporations become owners of portfolios of tradeable Integrated Value Systems.

Boards of directors become boards of advisors: Responsibilities will be realigned in accordance with new corporate legal entities and structures.

Middle managers awarded new level of responsibility: As authority, ownership and control is refocused on Integrated Value Systems, a greater gap will emerge between senior and middle management. Senior leaders will oversee the management of entire portfolios of value systems. Although recognised as senior executives, middle managers will be responsible for the performance of the value systems and the efficiency and effectiveness of 'agile' teams operating within those value systems. Under this scenario, you can expect

- businesses at the portfolio level will evolve from small businesses into more substantive ones, and
- as value system portfolios evolve, they will be spun off and then split into new value systems.

New organisation structures: Corporations will be tech heavy, agile, global and spatial (interested or involved in outer-space venturing). Head offices will be reduced to the CEO, close (strategic) advisors and analytics/artificial intelligence specialists. The head office will oversee or be a part of the management of a portfolio of Integrated Value Systems, as opposed to portfolios of brands or business units. At this level, we can expect the strategy function to be very strong and as a part of that, as explained in the T-wI case study explored in the fieldbook that is a companion to this book, *Corporate Strategy (Remastered) II*, will be embedded with a central Corporate University entity.

New systems and processes will require a new take on culture: Culture will reside with each value system. When run as independent value systems, there will be an overriding understanding of issues of governance, values and purpose. The 'corporate culture' will differ between one value system and another. An influential culture will no doubt exert a degree of influence on each value system.

Legal, tax and compliance requirements will be fully automated: No value system will be too big or too small, all may be sold off, merged or closed down at any time.

Organisational learning will be the key to competitive advantage: Each portfolio of value systems will be aligned with and, ultimately, become an integral component of a formal corporate/organisational learning capability.

Corporate planners become strategy practitioners: An inevitable new focus – adoption of Third Wave Strategy with an emphasis on open strategy practice and focus on stakeholder (social issues) as much as shareholder (financial gain) value.

Strategy will be data driven, knowledge based and highly cognitive in its management: Knowledge informed by artificial intelligence and closed loop, but Integrated Value Systems will be the primary source of renewable competitive advantage. Clearly, Third Wave Strategy will have a critical role to play in a new era and new world of multidextrous, corporate opportunity seeking. The one thing that will drag on the progress of the outputs from Third Wave Strategy will be bureaucratic and outdated matters of corporate governance that have already become an inhibiter to progress in the business environment of today. That means that organisations must seek to break down rules and regulations that in many cases were designed and enacted in an era gone by and are of relevance to a world that is rapidly dying or no longer exists. Company and tax laws that corporations must comply with today are examples of areas where tradition and precedence dominate, outmoded modern-day practices and procedures.

Governance reform and the corporation of the future

We have referred previously to the report form the British Academy that has set out to establish a new framework for business in the 21st century. Regrettably, the research parameters unwittingly focused on the evidence of a firm's inability to 'adapt and respond' to change. Of course, as we now understand, for all this perspective brings, it implies an absence of prosponsive invention.

Even so, the insight the research does include contributes to a focus around these three areas, which we agree needs some attention. Similarly, they provide a grounding to a revised perspective of the age-old conundrum of finding the balance between the interests of the shareholders of the corporation versus those of the stakeholder. As a fundamental component of Purpose, Mission, Vision, it is essential that the strategy practitioner should be aware of the specifics of these issues of relevance to the business with which they are engaged in the strategising activities.

The report: the corporation of the future

In similar fashion to our *remastering* of strategy, the British Academy research team is ultimately seeking to *reconceptualise* the corporation of the future. The research leader, Professor Colin Mayer (2018), was afforded the help and support of 31 academics and 25 business leaders. Mayer's remit, he observed, was to "consider the implications of economic, environmental, political and social challenges, and scientific and technological opportunities for the future development of business". In his first report, he sought to identify a new framework for the contextual backdrop to a corporation. This framework, he suggested, would be focused on

> *a redefinition of corporate purpose that is distinct from shareholder returns, an establishment of trustworthiness founded on norms of integrity, and the embedding of a culture in organisations that enables both.*

We follow the three issues of purpose, trust and culture as the basis for our observations where solutions to the issues identified by Mayer can be addressed. In proposing a solution, we draw on evidence of existing practice or the application of Third Wave Strategy to practice.

Purpose as the basis for good governance

Issue: A relentless pursuit of profit, Mayer reported, has led to an "overzealousness and sometimes outright greed at senior levels". Mayor proposed that the solution to this is for a corporation to revisit its purpose. The objective would be to develop strategy that is accommodative of the needs of both shareholders and other stakeholders of the firm.

Sample solution: In our exploration of Third Wave Strategy, we have identified an imperative for an expression of purpose to be the foundation of strategy. To this extent, we have proposed in Chapter 5 the adoption of the practice whereby "strategy follows purpose, structure follows strategy, systems follow structure". It is up to practitioners to ensure that the definition of purpose incorporates the demand for shareholder and stakeholder interests.

Accountability and trust

Issue: Mayer expresses a strong desire that a greater degree of alignment should prevail between owners and managers of corporations. In a broader sense, we have identified three levels of alignment and discussed them at length in the last chapter (Chapter 5). Mayer's call for alignment is quite specific; we ask, however, can it be applied in a broader context at each level we discussed in Chapter 5.

Sample solution: As an example of an alternative form of ownership, we refer you to German industrial, engineering and technology company Bosch.

Since 1964, Bosch's majority shareholder has been Robert Bosch Stiftung GmbH. This is not an individual but a charitable foundation. The Stiftung is responsible for the continuation of the charitable and social endeavours of the company founder, Robert Bosch. It sees itself as a foundation that pursues its objectives both with programs and institutions of its own by supporting suitable projects and initiatives proposed by others for tackling challenges faced by society. Although this format goes a long way to resolving conflict between shareholder and stakeholder, there is a risk that this 'extended family' introduces a whole new set of parties whose interests must be addressed and catered to.

Commitment to core values and culture

Issue: The original purpose of a corporation according to Mayer was "to deliver a valuable service, not to simply make a profit". Too many corporations today, he observed, demonstrate perceptions of values that reflect "toxicity and greed".

Sample solution: Robert Bosch Stiftung GmbH is an example of an organisation that has adopted an opposite perspective of Governance. Another is the confectioner, pet care and general food producer Mars Inc. Employees at Mars are known as 'associates' rather than staff, as their culture is one of inclusiveness and shared values. Accordingly, Mars associates live and breathe an embedded core value that was first formulated by Forrest E. Mars Jr., a descendent of the founding father, Frank C. Mars. That value represents a code of conduct enunciated by the phrase "a mutuality of benefits for all stakeholders". Consistent with that value are five guiding principles. They are quality, responsibility, mutuality, efficiency and freedom. Every decision made by Mars associates has those core values front and centre in their minds.

Although Mayer's (2018) report provides scant attention to the impact of digital technology on the corporation of the future, it does provide a significant challenge to corporation's generally accepted modes of behaviour; their basis for, and purpose in, 'doing' strategy; and the reasons they exist. Too many corporations have been found to be wanting in this area. Third Wave Strategy was developed on a fundamental philosophy of creating an environment of change. It is grounded in a notion of open strategy practice, which, at the least, will provide a foundation upon which recognition, acknowledgement and subsequent depth of dialogue focused on change can take place. We discussed the concept of open strategy practice in Chapter 1. We explore it further here as we see it as key to both the future of strategy practice and an integral component of the corporation of the future.

Open strategy revisited: how to be what you can't see

The solution to the primary challenge for strategy practitioners in the future corporation can be resolved in the same way that was identified by Milbrey McLaughlin (2018). In her book *You Can't Be What You Can't See*, McLaughlin described how the Chicago Community Youth Creative Learning Experience (CYCLE) enabled hundreds of disadvantaged African American youths to be saved from poverty and generational unemployment. The underlying philosophy of CYCLE is highly consistent with that of Third Wave Strategy. It is to consistently

> *challenge current assumptions about the enduring effects of stasis and embedded perceptions of "what is" and instead: highlight the power of opportunity and thereby; imagine and take a different path.*

In the adoption of the proposal that we "imagine and take a different path", we suggest that it is now time to seriously consider and engage with the idea of open strategy practice.

Open strategy is highly consistent and sympathetic to the similar topic of open innovation. Openness, though, is not necessarily "an unalloyed good for organisations", according to Whittington et al. (2011). Its characteristics consist of two critical dimensions; both are intuitively beneficial in nature. The first is "inclusiveness, in other words the (broad) range of people involved in making strategy". Second is an openness in terms of "transparency, both in the strategy formulation stage and, more commonly, in the communication of strategies once they are formulated" (Whittington et al., 2011). In his presentation at a conference held in London (Strategic Management Institute International Conference, 2018), Whittington defined the notion of open strategy broadly as "a program of continual transition of strategy content, enabled through a new-found 'democratisation' of strategy". Open strategy practice is a complimentary and voluntary program to our formal Program of Continual Strategy Renewal (Chapter 4). It is also a natural fit with our proposed establishment of a formal community of strategy practice (Chapter 3). This is also complementary to Whittington's belief, as he also suggested it is akin to a phenomenon where communications about strategy content is "thrown open to internal and external stakeholders alike". In this brave new world, the setting of strategic objectives becomes very nimble as learning from open strategy practice is absorbed and acted upon very quickly.

To introduce the idea of open strategy, Whittington pointed to three forces of change. First is technology, and here he reminded us of the dramatic improvements in communication technologies as a key driver of change. Second is the evolution of the way we socialise and share information within and across newly defined (agile) organisation structures. Third is the transformation of organisational/corporate culture, whereby a degree of openness is now expected as the relaxing of social norms has led to an expectation of transparency in communications, especially in the area of strategy, which was once the sole domain of the corporate elite. Whittington left the audience with the following challenge: "Who will be the agents of open strategy practice?"

We accept that there is a degree of risk associated with the foregoing transformations and the introduction of Third Wave Strategy in its entirety. Accordingly, we have identified both positive and negative outcomes from various adaptive and inventive choices. We address these as follows within the context of corporate governance and strategic risk.

Corporate governance of the future: managing strategic risk

Consistent with the philosophy of evaluation, it is useful to understand the risks of the various 'sponsive' options available to the strategy practitioner. We consider these risk factors and structure them in accordance with another adaptation of the sponse matrix, as illustrated Figure 6.5.

Strategic risk and the degrees of strategically focused transformational change can be reviewed within the context of the sponse matrix on a quadrant by quadrant basis. In this application of the matrix, we explore the potential for risk to impact the organisations contained therein, with an emphasis on congruity. A congruous outcome is described as a successful outcome, which is realised either by luck (serendipity) or by design. An incongruous outcome is an unsuccessful one, realised as a result of bad luck or poor design.

Quadrant 1, Inertia: There is likely only one disappointing outcome from Inertia, with the final outcome being a matter of degree. At its best, supermarket chains/retailers, such as Tesco (UK), Coles (Australia) and Kruger (US), seem to have survived in a bubble of *stagnation* for many years. No one is expecting them to soar, and their history of decline is erratic. Sears, on the other hand, as we saw in Chapter 2, ebbed and flowed continuously between a state of *stagnation* and *decline* before finally entering bankruptcy. Even though

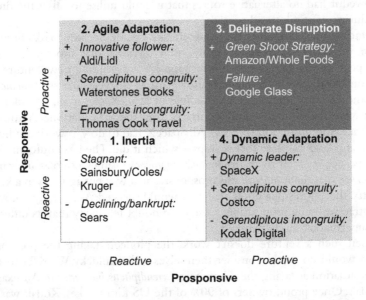

Figure 6.5 Matrix of risk assessments from sponsive strategic change

CEO Eddie Lampert invested significant sums of money while harbouring an expectation of revival, many pundits were not surprised when it finally did succumb to failure.

Quadrant 2, Agile Adaptation: There is a correspondingly disappointing outcome from the quadrant depicting the life of a static follower of change. As an adapter to 'what is', occupants of this quadrant are characterised as survivors. We have awarded them the title of *innovative followers*. Standout organisations are Aldi and Lidl. Each have survived and are taking market share from their rivals Tesco, Coles and Kroger. Having spawned a differentiated business format at the least and the lowest price at best, their ability to keep their business format fresh is the key to their long term survival and continue growth. This is still a quadrant of high risk though. The representation of a positive outcome from a notion of *serendipitous congruity* in this quadrant can be awarded to Waterstones bookstores, which, as we suggested in Chapter 5, demonstrates a capacity to invigorate a physical representation of transformation. This transformation saw it turn its bookstores into entertainment venues and redefined representations of merchandising while evolving a presence in online retailing.

One of the many corporations that have been unable to survive in this quadrant in recent times was Thomas Cook Travel, a travel agency that ultimately succumbed to its fate of *erroneous incongruity*. This company's attempt to adaptation via the launch of a Green Shoot accelerated Deliberate Disruption saw it create a cash flow crisis in the form of its purchase of an airline that ultimately drew it into a sudden death plunge. Although such an acquisition could have made sense from a Dynamic Market System perspective, Thomas Cook Travel had no competence in actually running an airline. This became obvious when it showed it had no alternative routes that it could utilise to offset the drop in sales during off-peak travel periods.

Quadrant 3, Dynamic Adaptation: As a sign of increasing risk but greater return, we explore further this prosponsive territory that also carries with it three possible outcomes. First is a prosponsive entry into a new venture with a reasonable degree of certainty, a move that is characteristic of *dynamic leaders*. Although very high risk, the example of SpaceX says it all. Founder Elon Musk was able to secure future contracts from the US's National Aeronautics and Space Administration (NASA). All SpaceX had to do was work out how to launch and land risk-free rocket ships – which it did. The next outcome is the circumstance we refer to as *serendipitous congruence*. Using Costco as an example, we can see that their venture was prosponsive in a way, but as it was in a known industry, there was still a good chance it would succeed. As a highly innovative and attractive value proposition, Costco no doubt felt lucky that its differentiated supermarket model worked.

When such a venture doesn't work, the pioneers taking the prosponsive option would no doubt consider themselves to be unlucky. We refer to firms in this situation as facing the dilemma of *serendipitous incongruence*. An example is Kodak. Once proud owners of 90% of the US film market, Kodak was well positioned to foresee the impact that digital technology would have on their industry (Dan, 2012). Accordingly, they became one of the first organisations to develop and introduce digital cameras. Unable to successfully transform to a new digital era, Kodak ended up abandoning the industry altogether.

Quadrant 4, accelerated, Deliberate Disruption: In the final quadrant, we have proposed the notion of Green Shoot Strategy. Although highly structured and well thought through, strategy practitioners must know that actions taken here will either work extremely well or not at all. The idea in the latter instance is to allow the Green Shoot to succeed or to fail fast before too much investment and lessons learned are lost following that failure. Amazon is the obvious story of success in this value-based system design. Sears is an obvious example of a less-fortunate outcome. When engaged in any form of Deliberate Disruption, it is always wise to ensure that you have access to a method of solid strategic risk.

Managing strategic risk: an alerting mechanism

In the management of strategic risk, we propose the use of the alerting mechanism illustrated in Figure 6.6.

Similar in concept to the alerting mechanism presented in Figure 5.4, the strategic risk representation is based on the principle that some of the projects initiated as an outcome from strategy will carry a greater degree of risk than others. Each quadrant carries different responses in accordance with the category of risk. These levels will range from major unforeseen emergencies to anticipated low-impact outcomes.

Will there be a fourth wave of strategy?

Amazon, now the standout operator of an Integrated Value System based fundamentally on an advanced and digitalised Core Competence Platform, was founded at the very beginning of the 4IR on 5 July 1994. Now recognised for its service offering in the fields of e-commerce, cloud computing, digital streaming and artificial intelligence, there is no doubt that the Bezos-led, strategy-focused S Team is far more advanced in its approach to strategy than many other corporations in the world today. That doesn't mean that Bezos and his team are any smarter than their compatriots in major corporations. It does mean that they have a capacity to think, act and lead differently, manage risk differently and drive change differently.

In this book, we offered a framework that will provide you with the means to structure your strategic thinking and, thereby, aid its reframing in the context of increasing uncertainty, complexity and volatility. We have also provided insight into an approach to putting the outcome from your newly contextualised strategic thinking into practice. This was presented as a Cycle of Organisational Transformation and Renewal, which in turn is informed by an associated Program of Continual Strategy Renewal. These mechanisms will provide you with the necessary fundamentals to commence the transformation of your corporation, business unit or division post haste.

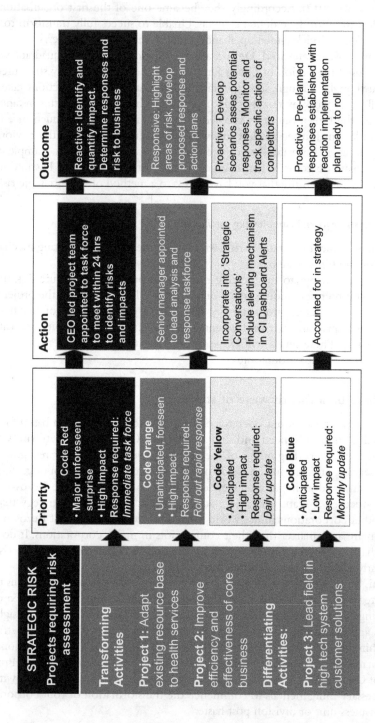

Figure 6.6 Strategic risk alerting mechanism

Third Wave Strategy, however, is not like a chemical formula that enables mass production of goods, such as soap, drugs or processed food, nor is it the same as a standardised formulaic process that enables the practice of accounting, engineering and architecture. It is an approach that prompts the need for useful and relevant data, a means to contextualise that data, interpret that data and turn it into knowledge and to then turn it into strategic intelligence.

So, yes, there will be a fourth wave of strategy, its development is already underway.

The greater the capacity for organisational learning, open strategy practice, artificial intelligence, deep-dive analytics and search in your organisation, the faster the Fourth Wave Strategy will evolve.

Final word: what are you waiting for?

Astronauts involved in the race to be first to the moon in the 1960s were prepared to give their lives in their endeavour to realise their purpose. Some, in fact, did. Against a backdrop of technology that was less sophisticated than a mobile phone, no one was deterred from the realisation of Purpose, Mission, Vision. Of course, no one would intend the pursuit of that endeavour to lead to such a tragic demise, and no one would be expected to take the risk to do so. But isn't that the point? There is a risk of failure in everything we do. No lives will be lost if corporations were to become more aggressive in their approach to the optimisation and even invention of future opportunity. So, what are you waiting for? There is still a long way to go with the 4IR digital technology, but it is much, much better than that available in the era of Apollo 11, and it is continuing to evolve and improve.

We hope the practices and praxis presented in our remastering of strategy will encourage you as a professional strategy practitioner to reframe, to think differently and to take action. Everyone knows that its difficult to be what you can't see, but your uptake of the concepts we have presented in the context of Third Wave Strategy will give you a head start. Our recommendation to all serious strategy practitioners is to

be bold, be brave but don't be reckless.

There is nothing reckless about the uptake of recommendations, methodologies and concepts discussed in this book. We invite you to indulge those who have described the experience as "taking their understanding of strategy to the next level". We wish you luck in your endeavours.

Bibliography

Allen, L., *Chocolate Fortunes: The Battle for the Hearts and Minds, and Wallets of China's Consumers*, AMACOM, New York, 2010

Amazon, www.aboutamazon.co.uk/uk-investment/our-principles-for-how-we-operate, 2019

Andrews, K.R., *The Concept of Corporate Strategy*, Dow Jones-Irwin, Homewood, IL, 1965

Ansoff, H.I., Strategies for Diversification, *Harvard Business Review*, 35(5), September–October 1957

Ansoff, H.I., *Corporate Strategy*, McGraw-Hill, New York, 1965

Baghai, M., Coley, S., & White, D., *The Alchemy of Growth*, Perseus Publishing, New York, 1999

Bariso, J., In Just 3 Words, Amazon's Jeff Bezos Taught a Brilliant Lesson in Leadership, *Inc. com*, April 13, 2017, www.inc.com/justin-bariso/it-took-jeff-bezos-only-three-words-to-drop-the-best-advice-youll-hear-today.html

Bolman, L.G., & Deal, T.E., *Reframing Organizations: Artistry, Choice and Leadership*, 6th Ed., John Wiley & Sons, New York, 2017

Bosch, Robert Bosch, www.bosch-stiftung.de/en/who-we-are

Breakthrough Starshot, 2017, https://breakthroughinitiatives.org/initiative/3

Calof, J.L., & Wright, S., Competitive Intelligence: A Practitioner, Academic and Inter-Disciplinary Perspective, *European Journal of Marketing*, 42, 2008

Carlson, R., *Don't Sweat the Small Stuff*, Penguin Random House, Australia, 2016

Chandler, A., *Strategy and Structure: Chapters in the History of the Industrial Enterprise*, MIT Press, Cambridge, MA, 1962

Chou, J., *New Cancer Hope Defies Gravity*, University of Technology (UTS) website, November 13, 2019, https://www.uts.edu.au/news/health-science/new-cancer-hope-defies-gravity

Colvin, G., What the Hell Happened at GE? *Fortune*, May 24, 2018, https://fortune.com/longform/ge-decline-what-the-hell-happened/

Cutter, C., Amazon to Retrain a Third of Its U.S. Workforce, *Wall Street Journal*, New York, Updated July 11, 2019 7:08pm ET, www.wsj.com/articles/amazon-to-retrain-a-third-of-its-u-s-workforce-11562841120

Dan, A., Kodak Failed by Asking the Wrong Marketing Question, *Forbes*, 2012, www.forbes.com/sites/avidan/2012/01/23/kodak-failed-by-asking-the-wrong-marketing-question/#e1a12383d470

de Gues, A.P., *Planning as Learning*, Harvard Business Review, Boston, MA, March–April 1988

de Gues, A.P. *The Living Company*, Harvard Business School Press, Boston, MA, 1997

de Waal, A.A., The Characteristics of a High Performance Organisation, Academic Director Centre for Organizational Performance, *Maastricht School of Management*, Maastricht, January 2010

De Wit, B., & Meyer, R., *Strategy Synthesis*, 4th Ed., South-Western Cengage Learning, Andover, United Kingdom, 2010

Doz, Y.L., & Kosonen, M., *Fast Strategy: How Strategic Agility Will Help You Stay Ahead of the Game*, Pearson Education, Harlow, 2008

Economy, P., *Richard Branson: 19 Inspiring Power Quotes for Success*, Inc. March 20, 2015, https://www.inc.com/peter-economy/richard-branson-19-inspiring-power-quotes-for-success.html

Emspak, J., What Is Augmented Reality? *Live Science*, June 01, 2018, https://www.livescience.com/34843-augmented-reality.html

Flood, R.L., *Rethinking the Fifth Discipline – Learning Within the Unknowable*, Routledge, New York, 1999

Ford Motor Company – *2017 Annual Report*, https://s22.q4cdn.com/857684434/files/doc_financials/2017/annual/Final-Annual-Report-2017.pdf

Ford Motor Company – *2018 Annual Report*, https://s22.q4cdn.com/857684434/files/doc_financials/2018/annual/2018-Annual-Report.pdf

Ford Motor Company: *Creating Tomorrow, Together. Ford Motor Company – 2018 Annual Report*, https://corporate.ford.com/content/dam/corporate/en/company/corporate-governance/2018-Annual-Report.pdf

Ghoshal, S., & Bartlett, C., *The Individualised Corporation – A Fundamentally New Approach to Management*, William Heinemann, London, 1999

Grant, R.M., *Contemporary Strategy Analysis and Cases: Text and Cases*, John Wiley & Sons, New York, 2016

Grove, A., *Only the Paranoid Survive: How to Exploit the Crisis Points That Challenge Every Company*, Doubleday, New York, 1999

Haden, J., Jeff Bezos Says 1 Thing Separates Successful People from Everyone Else (and Will Keep You from Giving Up on Your Dreams Too Soon), *Inc.com*, 2019, www.inc.com/jeff-haden/jeff-bezos-says-1-thing-separates-successful-people-from-everyone-else-and-will-keep-you-from-giving-up-on-your-dreams-too-soon.html

Hamel, G., & Prahalad, C.K., Competing for the Future, *Harvard Business Review*, July–August 1994

Hedley, B., *Strategy and the Business Portfolio*, Long Range Planning, London, February 1977, https://www.sciencedirect.com/science/article/abs/pii/0024630177900425?via%3Dihub

Hunter, P.W., *Strategic Revitalisation: A Strategic Business Model of Innovation and Growth*, Doctor of Business Administration Thesis, Graduate School of Business and Law, RMIT University, Melbourne, Australia, 2001

Jarzabkowski, P., & Spee, A.P., Strategy-as-Practice: A Review and Future Directions for the Field, *International Journal of Management Reviews*, 11(1), 69–95, 2009

Johnson, G., Whittington, R., Regner, P., Scholes, K., & Angwin, D., *Exploring Strategy*, Pearson, Essex, 2017

Kaplan, R., & Anderson, S., *Time-Driven Activity-Based Costing*, Harvard Business Review, Boston, MA, November 2004

Kim, W.C., & Mauborgne, R., *Blue Ocean Strategy: How to Create Uncontested Market Space and Make the Competition Irrelevant*, Harvard Business School, Boston, 2004

Kim, W.C., & Mauborgne, R., Value Innovation: A Leap into the Blue Ocean, *Journal of Business Strategy*, 26(4), 22–28, 2005

Kirby, J., & Stewart, T., The Institutional Yes, *Harvard Business Review*, October 2007

Kuchler, H., How Facebook Grew Too Big to Handle, *FT Magazine*, San Francisco, March 28, 2019, www.ft.com/content/be723754-501c-11e9-9c76-bf4a0ce37d49

Lane, R., Bezos Unbound: Exclusive Interview with the Amazon Founder on What He Plans to Conquer Next, *Forbes*, September 4, 2018

Levinson–King, R., & Palumbo, B., Donald Trump v the World: US Tariffs in Four Charts, *BBC News*, Toronto, December 3, 2018

Lewin, K., Frontiers in Group Dynamics: Concept, Method and Reality in Social Science: Social Equilibria and Social Change, *Human Relations*, 1, 5–41, 1947

Madhumita, M., & Waters, R., Google Claims to Have Reached Quantum Supremacy, *Financial Times*, September 21, 2019, www.ft.com/content/b9bb4e54-dbc1-11e9-8f9b-77216ebe1f17

Magretta, J., *Why Business Models Matter*, Harvard Business Review, Boston, MA, 2002

Mateja, J., How Chrysler Marriage Failed, *Chicago Tribune*, Chicago, IL, May 15, 2007

Mayer, C., *Reforming Business for the 21st Century: A Framework for the Future of the Corporation*, British Academy, London, November 2018

McLaughlin, M.W., *You Can't Be What You Can't See: The Power of Opportunity to Change Young Lives*, Harvard Education Press, Cambridge, MA, April 2018

Meyer, R.J.H., *Mapping the Mind of the Strategist: A Quantitative Methodology for Measuring the Strategic Beliefs of Executives*, ERIM Ph.D. Series Research in Management, Erasmus Research Institute of Management (ERIM), 2007

Mintzberg, H., & Waters, J.A., Of Strategies, Deliberate and Emergent. *Strategic Management Journal*, 6(3), 257–272, 1985

Murphy, H., FTC Approves $5bn Settlement with Facebook, *Financial Times*, San Francisco, July 13, 2019, www.ft.com/content/9dc13c84-a4eb-11e9-974c-ad1c6ab5efd1

Nalebuff, B.J., & Brandenburger, A.M., The Right Game: Use Game Theory to Shape Strategy, *Harvard Business Review*, 73(4), 57–71, 1995

Nicolaou, A., Amazon Becomes Fastest-Growing Music Streaming Service, *Financial Times*, New York, July 11, 2019, www.ft.com/content/60633178-a282-11e9-974c-ad1c6ab5efd1

Ohmae, K., *The Mind of the Strategist: The Art of Japanese Business*, McGraw Hill, New York, 1982

Opinion Lex, General Motors: Car Wars, *Financial Times*, November 26, 2018

Padmanabhan, G., The Future of Finance Is Augmented Intelligence and the New-Collar Worker, *Forbes*, July 12, 2018, https://www.forbes.com/sites/forbestechcouncil/2018/07/12/the-future-of-finance-is-augmented-intelligence-and-the-new-collar-worker/#61c24047ebe8

Parent, E., The Living Systems Theory of James Grier Miller. A Special Integration Group (SIG) of the International Society for the Systems Sciences (ISSS) Originally SGSR, Society for General Systems Research and IISII International Institute for General Systems Research for Systemic Inquiry and Integration, *The First International Electronic Seminar on Wholeness*, 2000, http://www.isss.org/primer/asem14ep.html

Patel, S., GE Power Falters on Underperformance of Alstom Investment, *Power Magazine*, November 2017, www.powermag.com/ge-power-falters-on-underperformance-of-alstom-investment/

Perry, J., *What Is Blockchain? A Primer on Distributed Ledger Technology*, January 4, 2017, IBM website, https://developer.ibm.com/dwblog/2017/what-is-blockchain-hyperledger-fabric-distributed-ledger/

Peters, T.J., & Waterman, R.H., *In Search of Excellence: Lessons from America's Best-Run Companies*, Harper & Row, New York, 1982

Peterson, H., Inside Sears' Death Spiral: How an Iconic American Brand Has Been Driven to the Edge of Bankruptcy, *Business Insider*, January 8, 2017, 8:41 am, www.businessinsider.com/sears-failing-stores-closing-edward-lampert-bankruptcy-chances-2017-1?r=UK

Porter, M., *Competitive Advantage: Creating and Sustaining Superior Performance*, The Free Press, New York, 1985

Porter, M., *On Competition*, Updated and Expanded Ed., Harvard Business School Press, Boston, MA, 2008

Prahalad, C.K., & Hamel, G., The Core Competence of the Corporation, *Harvard Business Review*, 68(3), 79–91, 1990

Rademakers, M., *Corporate Universities as Drivers of Organizational Learning*, Routledge, London, 2014

Rumelt, R., *Good Strategy, Bad Strategy*, Crown Publishing Group, New York, 2011

Safian, R., Ford CEO Jim Hackett on the Future of Car Ownership and Driving, *Fast Company*, September 1, 2018, www.fastcompany.com/40509038/ford-ceo-jim-hackett-on-the-future-of-car-ownership-and-driving

Schendel, D.E., & Hofer, C.W. (editors), *Strategic Management: A New View of Business Policy and Planning*, Little, Brown & Company, Boston, MA, 1979

Schumpeter, J.A., *An Inquiry into Profits, Capital, Credit, Interest, and the Business Cycle*, Harvard University Press, Cambridge, MA, 1934

Sears Archives, www.searsarchives.com/catalogs/questions/catalogend.htm

Sears Blog, Update on Our Transformation, September 13, 2018 by Eddie Lampert, https://blog.searsholdings.com/eddie-lampert/update-on-our-transformation/

Sears Holdings, Sears: Chairman's Letter to Shareholders, February 24, 2011, https://searsholdings.com/invest/chairmans-letters/february-2011

Sears Holdings, Sears: Chairman's Report, February 25, 2016, https://searsholdings.com/invest/chairmans-letters/february-2016; https://searsholdings.com/docs/investor/eap/q2-2018-earnings-release-presentation.pdf

Sears Holdings, Sears: Letter to Shareholders, Update on Our Transformation, September 13, 2018 by Eddie Lampert, https://blog.searsholdings.com/eddie-lampert/update-on-our-transformation/

Senge, P.M., *The Fifth Discipline: The Art and Practice of the Learning Organisation*, Doubleday/Currency, New York, 1990

Shubber, K., Group of US States Sue to Block T-Mobile's Takeover of Sprint, *Financial Times*, Washington, June 12, 2019

Shubhendu, S., & Vijay, J.F., Applicability of Artificial Intelligence in Different Fields of Life, *International Journal of Scientific Engineering and Research (IJSER)*, 1(1), September 2013

Smiknowledge and Strategic Management Institute (SMI) International Conference, Melbourne, October 2017 and London, November 2017, www.smiknowledge.com

Statista, The Statistic's Portal, www.statista.com/statistics/263264/top-companies-in-the-world-by-market-value/ (extracted 12.00 pm 23 January 2019)

Taleb, N., *The Black Swan: The Impact of the Highly Improbable*, 2nd ed., Penguin, London, 2010

Toyota, Company History, 2001, www.toyota-global.com/company/history_of_toyota/75years/data/conditions/philosophy/toyotaway2001.html

Trevor, J., & Varcoe, B., *A Simple Way to Test Your Company's Strategic Alignment*, Harvard Business Review, Boston, MA, 2016

Wack, P., Scenarios: Uncharted Waters Ahead, *Harvard Business Review*, September–October 1985

Walters, N., McDonald's Hamburger University Can Be Harder to Get into Than Harvard and Is Even Cooler Than You'd Imagine, *Business Insider*, 2015, www.businessinsider.com/McDonald's-hamburger-university-2333

Whittington, R., & Cailluet, L., The Crafts of Strategy: Special Issue Introduction by the Guest Editors, *Long Range Planning*, 41(3), 241–247, 2018

Whittington, R., Cailluet, L., & Yakis-Douglas, B., Opening Strategy: Evolution of a Precarious Profession, *British Journal of Management*, 22(3), 531–544, 2011

World Economic Forum, Fourth Industrial Revolution, https://www.weforum.org/focus/fourth-industrial-revolution

Index